RELENTLESS

*I Am Living Proof That There is
Always a Reason to Keep Fighting*

KADI HARNISH

Foreword by Dr. Bonnie Nussbaum
Afterword by Jennifer L. Napier, MA., LMFT

TITLETOWN
PUBLISHING

TitleTown Publishing, LLC
P.O. Box 12093 Green Bay, WI 54307-12093
920.737.8051 | titletownpublishing.com
Publisher: Tracy C. Ertl
Editor: Lori A. Preuss

Publisher's Cataloging-in-Publication
(Provided by Cassidy Cataloguing Services, Inc.).:
Names: Harnish, Kadi, author.
Title: Relentless : I am living proof that there is always
                a reason to keep fighting / Kadi Harnish.
Description: Green Bay, WI : TitleTown Publishing, [2024]
Identifiers: ISBN: 978-1-955047-44-9 (paperback)
                | 978-1-955047-26-5 (eBook)
Subjects: LCSH: Harnish, Kadi. | Sexually abused children--United
                States--Biography. | Adult child sexual abuse victims--
                Biography. | Adult child sexual abuse victims--Psychology.
                | Abused children--United States--Biography. | Victims
                of family violence--Biography. | Child sexual abuse--
                United States. | Rape--United States. | Incest--United
                States. | Sexual abuse victims' writings. | LCGFT:
                Autobiographies. | BISAC: SELF-HELP / Abuse. |
                FAMILY & RELATIONSHIPS / Abuse / Child Abuse.
Classification: LCC: HV6626.52 .H37 2024 | DDC: 362.76/40973--dc23

This book is dedicated to my daughter Annika,

For many years, I wondered why I was saved so many times, and the day I held you, I knew. I was always meant to be your Mom. I was always meant to love you. I was always meant to love you so you could change this world. You have saved me more times than I can count. Thank you for loving me unconditionally and giving me grace in all the moments when I needed it. You are everything beautiful in this world, wrapped into one perfect human, and this world is a brighter place because you exist in it.

I love you more than I could ever say.

Annika, 12 hours old

CONTENTS

CONTENT NOTE

Trigger warning for material contained in this book,
including sexual abuse and molestation, child abuse,
child-on-child abuse and molestation, abortion, suicidal
ideation, self-harm and cutting, and suicide attempts.

FOREWORD

Having invested almost 40 years of my working career into walking the healing path with survivors of some of the most unspeakable acts of sexual, physical, and emotional abuse experienced as children, I am so honored to have been asked to write the foreword for Kadi's beautiful book, *Relentless*. Kadi gives an eloquent voice to those who've endured childhoods of abuse, neglect, and trauma. Many survivors remain silent about what happened to them, some out of fear of retaliation, some convinced they won't be believed, some because they have not yet remembered. Kadi's ability to describe for non-abused people what the reality of an abused person is like is so valuable in breaking through the barriers to understanding and getting access to appropriate treatment for survivors.

As a clinical psychologist and holistic coach who specialized in trauma recovery, especially among those people with diagnoses other clinicians didn't want to work with, such as Dissociative Identity Disorder and Borderline Personality Disorder, I've been repeatedly traumatized myself by the lack of understanding and caring in the mainstream medical system and health insurance industry for people who've experienced more trauma than is even fathomable. I chose to leave mainstream healthcare after being told I was allowed three sessions to work with a woman who had experienced repeated stalking episodes perpetrated by a coworker, on top of a history of childhood abuse. Three sessions. We can do FAR better for our sisters and brothers who've been abused! To retraumatize people who've experienced abuse because they don't have the right kind of insurance or deep pockets to cover treatment costs or little or no access to trauma recovery providers is unconscionable! It is way past time to overhaul the systems that continue to fail our abused people, and books like Kadi's provide an opportunity for those who need to understand to get that deeper understanding necessary to make change occur.

Kadi also writes directly to those who have experienced abuse, such as she has, telling them they are beautiful souls and valuable to the world exactly as they are. She tells them they are not irreparably broken but compares them to the lovely Japanese art form known as Kintsugi or "golden joinery," in which pieces of pottery are put back together with gold or other precious metals, highlighting the repair, rather than hiding it. We "become strong in the broken places," to quote Ernest Hemingway, and the grace with which Kadi displays her own strength as she shares her story is validating for those of us who are survivors.

An unfortunate outcome of experiencing abuse is the smashing of our boundaries such that we become vulnerable to more acts of abuse. One way this occurs is the natural tendency in childhood to repeat and repeat and repeat that which is overwhelming to us in order to try to understand it. An example of this is a young boy whose father was killed in the terrorist attack on the twin towers. This child repeatedly pulled all the cushions and pillows off the sofa, hiding beneath them and sticking his hand up out of the "rubble" to be pulled to safety by family members at home. This scenario was played out over and over again as he worked to heal his trauma of losing his father. Imagine a sexually abused child repeating the same natural tendency, only to find that the outcome is not healing or different but more of the same abuse. Many have historically misunderstood this pattern, assuming either that the child "wanted" more abuse or not understanding why a child would put themselves back in harm's way, not realizing this repetition is a primary way children learn and try to understand that which is fearful and confusing.

Another way abuse becomes the "gift that keeps giving" through the smashing of boundaries is what a peer of mine so eloquently called "the wounded antelope syndrome." A predator in the animal kingdom is highly adept at discerning which member of the herd is vulnerable and, therefore, an easy kill. Human predators have the same capacity to read vulnerability in children and capitalize on that. I once had an offender I was treating casually remark that within a few minutes of observing children on a school playground, he could pick out who would be good victims. I share these stories to help the reader understand that children are not EVER responsible for the abuse that happens to them, despite behavior that might be misread as something other than fallout from abuse.

Kadi does a great job of articulating this kind of patterning both when she describes how her perpetrator told her this was what good girls do, this was love, and other manipulations to shift the onus of responsibility for the abuse from him to her and when she describes her attempts to get love through dressing provocatively and other behaviors. This does not mean she wanted more abuse; this means she was groomed to believe this was how one received love. Again, non-abused people so often misunderstand the actions of someone abused and unwittingly blame them for their abuse.

Kadi also offers some compelling descriptions of how memories of abuse can be locked away in the mind. In a subconscious attempt to survive the unthinkable, children's minds can encapsulate memories of the abuse until and if some trigger pierces that subconscious armor around them. Sometimes, pieces will trickle back to the surface; sometimes, the floodgates are blasted open. Regardless, it is often incredibly disorienting and disruptive to the life that was engineered so carefully as to protect the person living it from the horror of what happened. Because trauma memories tend to be fundamentally different than ordinary memories (either hazy and dreamlike or stark and vivid), many survivors and those who love them have a tendency to disbelieve those memories when they arise. Kadi's descriptions are so helpful in allowing survivors to realize the validity of what they've remembered.

If you, as a reader, are trying to understand why your own abuse happened or why someone who has been abused behaves as they do, Kadi's book will be an invaluable resource. Her discerning descriptions and unflinching narration of her own story serves as an excellent guide for understanding the complicated issue of child sexual abuse and recovery. May you emerge from having read Kadi's story with wisdom and compassion for those who have endured.

Dr. Bonnie Nussbaum
Clinical Psychologist and Holistic Coach

INTRODUCTION

Hi. I'm Kadi. I'm a mother, a fiancé, a daughter, a sister, a public speaker, an author, and a lover of all things sweet and all things sparkly. I will never pass by an animal without wanting to love it, and I will never pass up a free sample in the store. I care deeply and show it openly. I am extra, I am loud, I am vibrant, and I am so full of love.

Looking at who I am today makes it almost impossible to believe who I was years ago, and looking at what I'm doing now makes it almost unimaginable to believe what I went through then. That is the beauty in me. I am unexpected. I am messy. I am far less than perfect. But just when you think you can count me out, I take my white flag, wipe my sweat, and keep fighting.

I choose to share my story loudly and honestly because sometimes someone needs to see that it's possible. Maybe my story can be someone else's survival guide. Maybe, just maybe, I can make something beautiful out of the mess I was given. If I can help even one person, change even one life, then it is more than worth it.

Throughout our lives, we are faced with many opportunities to make a choice. A lot of these choices are small and cause very little change in our lives. Some of these choices, however, are massive and can alter the entire course of our lives. The moments that precede these decisions are often covered in emotions we don't yet know how to control: hatred, anger, guilt, pain, shame, etc. These emotions disguise them, and we often are so consumed by the feelings that we struggle to see the choice in front of us.

The best example I could give of this to illustrate how incredibly important these moments are is January 11, 2020. I was two days post hysterectomy and drowning in anger and confusion. I knew the abuse from my childhood played a massive part in my reproductive system failing and almost killing me, and I was angry that Astaroth had once again stolen something precious from me. I would never have another baby. I would never even have the choice. He had taken that from me, and I once again, felt broken, damaged, and worthless.

There I sat for the next few hours, staring at the empty wall, silent tears streaming from my face. 2 a.m. comes, and it's time for my next dose of pain meds. But what if I just took it all? I could be done with all of this. He would never be able to take anything from me again. I looked down at the bottle, my hands shaking, and at that moment, I didn't see it because I could see nothing but the pain and all that came with it. But I made a choice. I dumped the pills down the toilet, lied on the couch, and cried myself to sleep.

While I have never told anyone this, not my parents, not my now fiancé, I knew it wasn't a healthy thought, so I chose to go without any narcotics for the duration of my recovery until I knew I was in a well enough state to not risk that again.

Looking back, it's plain as day to see that I made the choice to keep fighting, and now, I am so grateful I did.

I can look back throughout my entire life and see all the moments of pain, anger, shame, etc., that washed over me, drowning me in trauma. These are the moments that preceded massive life choices, and they were usually brought on by something out of my control. We're going to call those WAVES.

I, then, can see the moments ripe with choice that follow all of those WAVES, those moments where everything has come to a head, and I have only two directions to go: give up or keep fighting. Those were the moments where my decision shaped the course of my life. We're going to call those PEAKS.

We all experience WAVES and PEAKS in our lives. Call them what you want. You have them, too. It's just part of the roller coaster of life. They're where growth happens, and strength is born. They're where we learn the toughest lessons, although we often don't appreciate them for what they are until much later. (Hello to this book).

Now, how many times have you confided in someone or vented to someone about something hurtful or traumatic, and their response has been something along the lines of, "It only hurts as long as you let it?"

Ouch. What the hell? I know. Believe me, I get it. But what if I told you that although the approach may seem abrasive, they're right?

I'm not taking away the time or strength it takes to heal. Not at all. In fact, I'm highlighting that. No, we can't just wake up one day and choose to "not be hurt" anymore. That's not reality. However, we can learn to recognize the WAVES and PEAKS so we can use them to our advantage.

Waves are out of our control. They are the abuse someone has put us through or flashbacks of the traumatic experiences we've lived through that we have to just survive. We can't change those. However, if we can learn to recognize them when they happen, we will then know that a PEAK is coming. If we can just hang on and keep our heads above water through the wave, we will find ourselves breathing again. We will be at the top, in the calm, and we will have an opportunity to take back control.

When I held that bottle of pills in my hands and considered ending all of the pain, I was allowing my trauma, my abusers, and my past to still have control over me.

WAVE.

When I chose to dump that bottle and focus on making it through that night, I decided I wasn't going to be another suicide statistic. I rose above the pain, and I took control back.

PEAK.

I originally intended this book to be only WAVES and PEAKS. However, as it has grown and taken on a life of its own, I have realized there was much more of my story that needed to be told. So, I will be sharing many of my WAVES and PEAKS with you throughout, as well as the parts in between that are necessary.

Now, I am mostly an open book about my life, my choices, and my healing. I am no longer ashamed of anything I have been through or any of the choices I have made. However, I am choosing not to name my abusers. I have been asked a lot, "Why?" My only answer is that while I understand there is power in naming your abusers and releasing that fear, I am no longer in a place where I have any desire to speak their names. I have taken back my power and my voice and am wholly unwilling to ever let them have it again. This is a story about me. This is about my journey, about my strength, about what I have overcome. I want the focus to remain on the beauty that these pages hold. This is not a story about the evil or depravity that exists in this world.

And with that, we begin.

THE FIRST ABUSER

Most of my flashbacks and trauma stem from this man and the things he did to me. Although I knew I would not name him in this book, I struggled for years to find the right title for him. Nothing seemed to fit just right. It felt impossible to describe all that he was in just one word. I looked at names for the devil. I researched ancient words that meant evil and vile. I almost settled on just calling him "Abuser 1".

And then, it clicked. Why was I giving him this energy and time? He didn't deserve an actual name, and I deserved to share my story with no regard for him.

So, I regretfully introduce you to "Astaroth." (Yeah. That's perfect.)

Astaroth was "A pillar of the community" and someone very close to our family. He was successful and well-liked. He was a businessman with a well-known name and plenty of money. On the surface, he seemed like a truly great man. In fact, I'm sure that those who never got to know the real him would defend him and his character to the death.

I first met him when I was a very young girl, sometime in my toddler years. Because I was so young, I don't remember much of the beginning. As I'm sure you understand from your own life, my memories

Kadi, 8 months old

5

of those younger years are not complete. They are individual moments that left lasting impressions on my subconscious in some way. Like the first real fight I remember my parents having. I can't tell you what was said or what it was even about, but I remember putting some of my stuffed animals into garbage bags because they were "divorcing" (whatever that meant) and didn't want to be without them, no matter where I ended up.

Astaroth was a handsome man who made me feel safe and loved. He was kind and giving. At least, that's what I thought in the beginning. What he truly was a predator. A predator who preyed on people, namely women, who had been stuck in a cycle of abuse since their childhood. He would earn their trust in order to gain access to their young daughters. (I say daughters instead of children because the only other child victims of his that I have talked to are girls). He was a cunning, charming man who was exceptionally good at manipulating anyone necessary, adult or child.

Now, before I go any further, I want to state once and for all that I do not blame my parents, my brothers, or any other adult in my life at all. And I will not accept anyone else placing blame on them either. We have all spent long enough blaming ourselves and sometimes even each other. We have worked so hard to heal past that and place the blame where it truly lies. So, unless you lived through this situation and experienced firsthand how adept this man was at getting what he wanted, you get no vote here. It was no one's fault but his. End of story.

Kadi, 2 years old

Astaroth was the only abuser who would lay his hands on me more than once. He would be a physical part of our lives for over ten years and would not be "gone" until I was a teenager.

The first few years were, as I said before, gaining our trust, helping our family, and making himself an important asset to our family, a "part of the family." We loved him. I loved him. He was in.

Kadi 4 years old

That was the first step in his master plan. The next step was to groom me over time. In order to stay a part of our lives long-term, he needed to move slowly. He needed to move our relationship closer to that of a sexual nature without anyone noticing. He couldn't continue if he was caught. He was playing the long game, and he was playing it well.

If you could sit down and watch this play out on a movie screen, you would see the same man who took me fishing and helped tie my shoes hurt me in the most unspeakable ways. The beginning of our relationship would seem so beautiful and wholesome, in stark contrast to the end.

It would progress from no physical contact to holding my hand while crossing the street, to his hands on my waist to spin me

Kadi, 2nd grade

around, to "cuddling," and so on. Always, the message was the same, "thank you for being such a good girl. You're doing so well". I may not remember every second of the day to day, but I will never forget his words. They pierced me every time he touched me in any way, and they became his greatest weapon. Those words held his power; he knew exactly when and how to wield them.

Those words of approval, affirmation, and manipulation paved his way, seemingly effortlessly, through the secret grooming of me to the first time he would REALLY hurt me and beyond.

We are about to get into the nitty gritty, and as I said earlier, I don't hold back when sharing. So please heed this warning. If you are triggered at all by mentions or details of SA, please read the rest of this book carefully. I will be sharing the very raw, intimate account of some of the abuse I endured, and I fully understand how triggering it can be.

Have your support plan in place. Be ready with healthy coping mechanisms. If necessary, let a trusted person know you will be reading this and may need them. This book is meant to heal, not hurt. So please, take care of yourself.

Do you remember the first time?

It was just supposed to be more "cuddling." I had become used to that. It didn't take you very long to convince me that the way it made my stomach twist and rot was normal. It didn't take many "This is what good girls do" to make me believe that you finding pleasure in taking off my clothing was okay.

But this time wasn't like all the rest.

Kadi, 8 years old

You quickly realized this wasn't enough for you anymore. Your "gentle" touches just didn't do it for you, did they?

Do you remember the first time?

Every tear that streamed down my face left a streak in the dirt that covered my cheeks. Just minutes ago, I had been outside catching grasshoppers, pretending I was a normal child.

Those tears washed the dirt down into my mouth, and I choked when I would desperately try to breathe.

Every time your skin touched mine, my skin crawled, and I winced in terror.

I fought so hard.

At first, I thought my tiny body harbored enough strength to hold you off of me. I was sure that if I told you I loved you enough, you would see that it was hurting me. You would definitely stop, then.

But you didn't.

Do you remember the first time?

That was the beginning of you taking what wasn't yours. The start of you robbing me of things I would never get back. The first time, I thought to myself, "Love is supposed to hurt."

I remember the first time.

The way the lamp light danced on the wood laminate wall. The smell of decay inside that old couch when you shoved my face deep into it so no-one would hear my cries for you to stop. The moment I realized your smile would never bring me joy again.

I remember the first time.

The way you exploded with anger when I bled. After all, that was the most I would ever bleed. You were more violent later, but that was when you broke me. The way that anger turned to joy as you watched every innocent piece of me leave my body and float into your hands.

I remember the first time.

I can't tell you how long it lasted. I can't tell you how long I screamed until my voice turned hoarse. I don't know how many of my "Please stop. I love you's fell on deaf ears. The only thing I was sure of at that moment was that this first time wouldn't be the last time. You didn't have to say it. My broken soul just knew.

Do you remember the first time?

Does it haunt you the way it does me?

It's hard for me to say exactly when that flashback was about. I don't have an exact date for any of this. But I do remember that the leaves were changing color the first time he put his hand on my thigh and smiled at me as if to set the example that I, too, should feel joy from his touch. I remember the sweat beading down my back from the blistering sun the first time he told me it was "our little secret." I do remember the frigid air feeling like razorblades in my lungs during every breath the first time he REALLY hurt me.

You see, between infantile amnesia and retrieving these memories after having repressed them for years, I may not be able to give you an exact date, but I CAN tell you exactly what I saw, smelled, heard, and tasted in every moment of every memory. I CAN tell you exactly what I was wearing and where we were. I will never forget the things that were done to me and the vivid details surrounding them.

Kadi and Kathi (mom) on 18th birthday trip

I was a very small child when Astaroth's reign of terror began. As I said before, he followed the typical pattern of a child predator. He chose me. He proved "trustworthy." He showered me with attention and gifts, and then he began to isolate me and implement his control. He slowly turned the seemingly innocent relationship we had into that of a sexual nature. The first time he "abused" me wasn't the first time he raped me. He abused me every time his hand brushed my cheek and made me shudder. He abused me every time he praised me for obeying him or threatened me if I told anyone our secrets. He abused me every time he thought of me as anything other than a small, innocent child.

It has taken me years to understand that it is okay for me not to remember certain things. I have had to be told time and time again that I was a CHILD, and my mind was protecting me by filing these times away in the almost unreachable parts of my memory. He brainwashed me into thinking no one would ever believe me if I told, and the erratic recalling of repressed memories only reinforced that belief at the beginning of my healing. I stayed quiet, telling only my EMDR therapist about these horrors as they flooded back. I essentially continued to keep Astaroth's secrets, intending to protect myself but still protecting him.

In a court of law, there has to be proof beyond a reasonable doubt of the "who, what, when, where, and why" to prove someone guilty. The timeline has to be solid (which means repressed memories won't cut it). What good would it do to tell anyone outside of that therapy room about what had happened to me? I didn't want to relive it for any reason other than finally healing from it for good. I didn't want to be barraged with questions I didn't have an answer for at the time. My greatest fear was for him to be proven right and for others not to believe me. He would remain a "pillar of the community," and I would still be the "little girl who lies for attention."

My subconscious, my mind, my beautiful little brain, did its best to protect me from unspeakable pain. Without that, I don't know if I would have survived. I don't think these memories were ever meant to surface. I think they were intended to stay locked away for good so I could continue to move on with my life as if nothing had ever happened. But they were a monster locked away, waiting for the moment the cage holding it would begin to wear. And as soon as it saw the bars begin to rust and weaken, it opened the flood gates and consumed all I was with its anger, hatred, pain, confusion, and bitterness.

I began writing what would eventually become this book just as a means to survive. When I would be overtaken with a flashback, I would write it out. Being able to see it on paper and physically in my hands made me feel as if I had control back. I felt as though I was in charge of how the story went. I never intended to share those pieces with anyone else, let alone publish them for the whole world to read. But I now stand strong in these truths,

1. My experience, although horrifying, is not unique. The number of victims of sexual abuse, specifically as a child, is far greater than the number of those who haven't experienced it.

2. Many of those victims are still trying to find their voice, and I can help them by sharing mine.

3. My experience is not any less real because I was a child who repressed the memories. No one gets to invalidate me because of what I did to SURVIVE.

Every day, as I lean further into my healing, I believe more and more that part of my purpose on this earth is to help others like me who are struggling to see the light. I choose to share my story now, hoping it will reach every single person who so desperately needs to see that they can and should still fight, that they can and will come out the other side victorious. I want to show them that while the journey is long and strenuous, the victory is that of legends past. I want YOU to look at me and what I have overcome and whisper to yourself, maybe even for the first time, "I can keep going."

Outside of his abuse, I was a normal child. I loved being outside and playing make-believe. I started dance very young and quickly fell in love with it. I learned to read very early and loved The Berenstain Bears. I was a beautiful, vibrant miracle of a child, and I want to take this opportunity to honor her.

Kadi, Kindergarten

Although my book focuses mostly on Astaroth, there were others who abused me sexually. And I think it is also important to share their part in my story.

THE SECOND ABUSER

He was a boy who lived up the street, who couldn't have been more than a year or two older than me. He was 7 or 8, and I was 6. Before I explain what happened, I want to make it very clear that I know, without a doubt now, that he had been abused in some form. He was a child who had been shown things and put through things he never should have. No one ever told me this. But I now know that is the reason why young children "experiment" in this way, exposing other children to things much too grown for them. He was a child. He was a victim. But this was also the first time I was sexually abused. I understand now that all of those truths exist in the same space.

Kadi 5 years old

All of his siblings were friends with mine, as well as all the other kids in the neighborhood. We were like a large family of misfit kids who would pal around together in the summer while our parents worked. We would play flashlight tag late into summer nights. We would spend the long summer days pooling money for the gas station or ice cream truck. We spent more time together than we did apart, and it was honestly some of the best memories of my childhood.

But then, one summer day, we were all going to go swimming, so we all met at their house to travel to the pool together. While coolers were being packed and towels were being shoved into beach bags, the boy invited me into his room. I followed him down the hall, excited to get everything ready so we could enjoy our summer day. Once we were inside his room, he did what every young child does and began to excitedly show me his newest toys and the posters on his wall that he had just gotten for his birthday. Everything was so innocent, so normal, so like it always had been, until it wasn't. Our older siblings began yelling from the kitchen that it was time to go. They were packed, had everything ready, and were eager to start the long trek before the sun was at its highest. The boy yelled back that he still needed to change, so our siblings said they would take everything and meet him outside when he was finished.

Before I could walk out of the room to join him, the boy shut his door and began to take off his clothing. As any embarrassed young girl would, I turned away and covered my eyes. I had never had a young boy undress in front of me before, but I understood privacy, especially when it came to boys, as I had two older brothers. Hands over my eyes, face in the corner, I felt my swimsuit strap being pulled down. As I reached up to move his hand and replace my strap, he said that he wanted to "explore" and that it would "feel really good."

I want to clearly state that while there was abuse, he did not rape me. I am choosing not to share the specific details of what happened that day because I do not want any part of this to guilt or shame the boy. I believe whatever you put into this universe, through your actions and words, comes back to you tenfold. So, although he may never read this, I will not speak of him as though he was something

I know he was not. He, clearly, had been abused. So, I only want to speak of him in the accurate light of what he was: another child victim. Someone had taken from him, and that cycle continued in his room that day.

The next few years were sadly filled with less innocence as Astaroth continued to take from me. I did my best to maintain a normal childhood, at least in the sense that I knew how. I loved to hang out with my friends. We would often go to the bowling alley, especially in the summer. They offered all school-age kids one free game every day through summer break, so most of my school was there daily, working towards a perfect 300. We also spent a lot of time at our city "pool." I put that in quotations because it was less of a pool and more of a large natural pond. There were two diving boards and an area roped off for lap swimming. But nothing was concrete or chlorinated. It was all dirt and algae, and we loved every bit of it. We would dare each other to do the best belly flop off the high dive and would immediately regret taking that dare. Kids would often come out of the water squealing from the insects or fish that surprised them and would sometimes end up with "swimmer's itch." But it was irreplaceable. We could be crazy, be free, and be kids. This was our refuge from the heat and problems at home, and we loved it and all of its imperfect glory.

I continued to dance, taking every class I could, from jazz to tap, hip-hop, and ballet. I did group performances as well as solos and duos. I looked forward to our recitals every year and found an escape I desperately needed in our practices. I spent more and more time in the studio every year and did my best to balance school, home, and dance.

I was not a "cool kid" in school. As a matter of fact, I was a crybaby and a weirdo. Or, at least, that's what the other kids said. I craved approval and attention from boys so badly that I would often embarrass myself in front of all of the other students. I remember a time in fourth grade when we had show and tell. The other kids brought their pets, cool bikes, or scooters, but what did Kadi bring? Well, it was a love poem that she wrote about the most popular boy in all of fourth grade who would clearly never like her back. Oh, but that's not all. She didn't just bring it to school. She read it in front of the whole class and even dedicated it straight to him. Needless to say, it was not received the way I had hoped, and that moment cemented my place in "Weirdo History." But I craved attention and love from boys so fiercely that even that couldn't stop me.

In fifth grade, I began wearing makeup and hiding miniskirts in my purse so my Mom wouldn't know what I wore to the movies with my friends. I became almost obsessed with boys and began making very unsafe and unsmart decisions. I "made out" with a boy for the first time at an age far too young and was actively seeking "relationships" with boys much older. And this is exactly what created the perfect situation for someone much older to take advantage of me.

THE THIRD ABUSER

Sometimes, when I reflect on what he did to me, I feel as though it was the most confusing and damaging instance of abuse I had been through. I don't know how to explain it. You may not understand why I would even consider this because, in comparison to some of the other things that had been done to me, this seems so much "less." Honestly, I can't really answer that for you except just to reiterate that what someone on the outside of sexual abuse sees is only the surface, the physical, the very tip of the iceberg of the damage. For those of us who experienced it, the largest part of our battles come from thoughts, damage, and brokenness unseen.

Kadi, 10 years old

I was 10. He was 14. He was my best friend's older brother. He was abrasive. He was rude. He was in and out of juvie for a slew of crimes. But he paid me attention, and as I've shared before, I CRAVED that. It began with all of us hanging out in a big group, where he would make comments about what I was wearing or how he liked how I did my hair. After a few months, it escalated to him holding my hand, wrapping his arms around me, and calling me his "girlfriend." The first time I stayed the night at my friend's house after he "picked" me was when the months of things kind of just simmering came to a boiling point. There were no adults present, and there wouldn't be until late the next morning, although we had told my Mom that wasn't the case. Although I had no idea he would be there that night, as he was usually out partying with his friends, I wasn't concerned when I walked in and saw him. After all, he was my "boyfriend," and he was cool, and he was older, a bad boy, and "loved" me.

The night began like a normal sleepover. My friend and I watched Justin Timberlake's music videos, pretending to be his backup dancers. We curled each other's hair and ate frozen pizzas. We were normal 10-year-olds. And then, so quickly, things changed. Her brother invited me into his room to watch movies and "smoke pot." And while I didn't do drugs, I didn't want to be "uncool," so I accepted the invitation and followed him into his room. As the door closed behind me, I felt this sense of unease wash over me. I couldn't have explained it then, but I knew this was not somewhere I should be, and these are not things I should be entertaining.

As we sat on his bed, I came up with excuses to refuse his offers for marijuana, but when it came to his physical advances, I ignored that sick feeling in the pit of my stomach and just told myself that it was okay. He began by kissing me, and when I tried to pull away, he pinned me down and began to run his hand up my shirt. I became uncomfortable and tried to pull my shirt down and stand up, but he was much bigger than I was, and his weight made it impossible to stop him without causing a scene. The last thing I wanted was to be "uncool" and make him not love me anymore, and since he wouldn't stop, I decided to just go with it. He undid his belt and unbuttoned his pants. He then stood in front of me as if I wasn't ten years old, and the sight of him in his faded plaid boxers suddenly made me *really want* to take part in whatever he had in mind.

He then walked toward me and, once again, smothered me with the weight of him, touching me and kissing me. I was uncomfortable, but I could deal with this if it would make him love me. But then, he told me to put my mouth on his penis. Those weren't the words he used, but you get the picture. I don't know why this caused such a drastic reaction from me. After all, I had already been put through this by Astaroth. You would think there was nothing that would shock me, but this did. I couldn't do it. I told him I couldn't and I wouldn't do it. He became angry, and I began to cry. I was ruining everything. He didn't love me anymore, and I was useless. I had heard those words before. I wanted to be loved. I wanted to be "good." But I couldn't bring myself to "please him" in the way he wanted.

He angrily dressed himself and yelled at me to get out of his room and out of his house. As he yelled that he never wanted to see me again, I crumpled on his front porch, so angry with myself that I ruined this and heartbroken that he no longer wanted me. He then slammed the door in my face, and I spent what remained of the night outside. I couldn't go home. Even if the distance were less, there's no way I could explain why I walked home in the middle of the night without giving all the details that I was less than proud of. When my ride showed up the next morning, I smiled and hid this away just as I did with so many other necessary secrets.

As I said before, I sometimes consider this the most damaging and confusing instance of abuse I have been through. It took me over 15 years to understand that this was, in fact, abuse. I was not "asking for it," nor did I cause it to happen. I was a young girl manipulated and groomed by a much older boy. Although he was still technically a minor, his intentions and tactics were, and are, clear as day. He took from me and then had me thinking I was "just a slutty girl" for years after.

REIGN OF TERROR

For the next couple of years, Astaroth continued his reign of terror. I would find any way possible to keep at a distance while also craving his approval and love. I knew what he did hurt me, but I had been programmed to believe that it was my fault. I would stop hurting and be "good enough" when I finally learned how to please him.

As you can imagine, this caused all sorts of destructive behaviors. I would lie frequently about anything and everything, just for attention. I would continue to dress and act inappropriately. I was screaming for help while still keeping so many secrets.

I found ways to escape the hell that I called life. I had dance. I had friends. I spent hours outdoors, too "busy" to spend time with Astaroth. One of the most heartbreaking realizations I have had in my healing is the answer to the question, "Why did you only take baths for so long when you were clearly old enough to shower?"

A shower only took me 15 minutes, maybe 30 at most. And then I was no longer "busy." But a bath. A bath could take HOURS if I did it right. Obviously, he couldn't come in the bathroom while I was in there, so this was the perfect escape. I would take my CD player and my Mom's Matchbox 20 CD, and I would stay as long as possible until the water was ice cold and wouldn't run hot anymore and until my fingers and toes were as wrinkled as a prune.

I created a world where he couldn't touch me, a refuge. It would help me disassociate during the instances of abuse in order to protect myself. I first rediscovered this world during one of my flashbacks of his abuse.

MY REFUGE

Your fingertips trace my jaw, following the tear that escaped as I closed my eyes- trying to find my refuge. It's the one place you can't find me.

I can feel the dew on the blades of grass under me and smell the lilacs in the distance. There's a beautiful yellow butterfly warming its wing in the late summer sun.

RIIIIIIIIIIIPPPPPPP

My refuge tears in two, opening to show you- your blue eyes, pools of black. A drop of sweat falls from your forehead, landing perfectly in the center of your hand that's covering my mouth.

I squeeze my eyes shut, desperately trying to repair the veil that separates me from reality.

Tears stream down my face, and I imagine a steady stream flowing next to me, crystal clear, carrying all of the golden and auburn leaves to their final resting place. I walk towards the sound of children playing. Their worlds are still intact-still completely innocent. Their joy washes over me, so pure-so whole.

RIIIIIIIIIIIPPPPPPP

It falls away again. Darkness floods in, so heavy, so cold. The air is stale. It chokes me as I try to breathe.

How do you breathe so freely?

I feel your grip tighten on my mouth.

"Yes. That's what I want. You're..."

I beg for my refuge to take me back as your words fade into a gentle breeze passing by. The sun kisses my cheeks as I look at the sky.

There's so much peace here. So much beauty in the world I've created.

I lie down in the grass once more. The shade from the old oak tree is my favorite resting place. A movie dances across the sky in the clouds. The princess outsmarts the dragon yet again. I close my eyes to drift off to sleep.

I wake on the still cold floor.

The room still dark.

The air still stale.

But somehow, less so.

When I realize you are gone, a smile crosses my face.

The princess may still be locked in her tower, but there will be no feast for the dragon tonight.

I CAN STILL HEAR HER

Editorial note:
Trigger warning for self-harm and cutting.

The year that I turned 13 was full of changes. Astaroth's place in our lives and our family has been revoked. He made some massive mistakes, and although he was not caught abusing me, he got caught hurting others, which ended up in us doing our best to make sure that he would no longer have any contact with us.

There were a lot of other big changes as well. It's now just my Mom and me. We moved to a new home. We are fighting for a fresh start. My Mom's chronic fatigue, which she had been battling since before I was born, has become worse, but she still does everything she can to provide for us. She is working odd jobs to pay our bills and cleaning the dance studio to pay for my lessons. There were days when she "wasn't hungry" or had "already eaten" just to make sure there was enough for me. I watched other Moms who were "normal" only give their kids a fraction of their time and energy, while I watched my Mom, who only had a fraction of what's "normal," give it all to me. I thank God every day for that woman and her strength. She set the example for me of a fighter and survivor and deserves more credit than she gives herself for where I am today.

Despite our efforts to be okay, I struggled with severe depression and anxiety. I had actually been diagnosed with many things many times over the years, but it wasn't until my teenage years that they took center stage.

Kadi, 8th grade

My Mom was now remarried to an incredible man who loved me like his own. Although my biological Dad and I struggled in our relationship (mainly because of my actions as a troubled kid), he fought hard to remain a part of my life and to show me how much he loved me. All of the memories of the sexual abuse were repressed, but symptoms of them showed clearly on the surface. I was still very much "the weird kid," probably even more so than before. I was bullied incessantly, and at 13, I began self-harming. It started as eraser burns but eventually turned into me taking apart every razor so I could hide blades in any place I would need them. I needed control. I needed to feel pain by my own hand instead of someone else's.

As time went on, I would give in to the urge to hurt myself more and more often. I wore only long sleeves, usually oversized hoodies, and I continued to seek attention in any way possible, which led to more bullying, which then led to more self-harm, and thus, I was stuck in a seemingly impossible cycle.

During my 8th grade year, I faced one of my greatest hardships but also experienced one of the most life-changing displays of love I would ever know.

I was 13. I walked into school for what I had planned to be my last day alive. I had made a plan to take my life that afternoon. Everything was ready. My plan was in motion. I had spent weeks fighting these thoughts and trying to convince myself there was another way, but I had lost all hope. All I had to do was make it through this one last day, and it would all be over.

It was only 2 hours until the end of the day when I was called into the office. Instantly, I was ushered into the counselor's office, where I was offered a bottle of water and a snack. I took the bottle of water, but not to drink. I just needed something to keep myself from fidgeting nervously. I could not give my plan away.

"I'm the guidance counselor for this school, but you can call me Daryce," a woman said in an intentionally soothing tone.

I didn't move her eyes from the tiny speck of blue paint on the carpet.

"Do you have any idea why you're here?"

Her voice was so comforting that I almost wanted to reach out for help one last time.

Her eyes still didn't move.

"Someone came to me very concerned about you. They care about you very much, and they said they saw some marks on your arm that might not have been accidents?"

I scoffed. There was no-one in this school that cared about me and especially didn't care about me cutting. They didn't care about the awful things I had been through. They all just made fun of me and called me a drama queen and attention whore.

"Can you pull up your sleeve for me?" Daryce asked as she inched closer, preparing herself for what she was about to see.

I stared harder at the blue spot on the carpet, wishing it was an ocean I could fall into and drown.

"Can I lift up your sleeve?"

I froze completely. I could feel my heartbeat in my throat.

Daryce tried to hide her gasp as she lifted my sleeve. My arm was littered with cuts, bruises, and burns, all in different stages of healing.

The flood gates opened.

I began to sob as I revealed my plan and explained all of the marks on my arms. Daryce listened intently.

"I'm going to get you help." She promised.

She made a few calls, the first being to my Mom. Before the end of that day, I was admitted to an inpatient treatment center, where I would spend the next two weeks.

I went through intense therapy, both individually and with a group. My family showed up for every family therapy session, and I participated fully in everything asked of me, which is probably why I was released in two short weeks, far shorter than the average.

I know what you're probably wondering, "Why didn't this intense therapy bring up any of my repressed memories?"

My only answer is that my subconscious wasn't ready to let them go yet. And thank God for that because it would have killed me to try to process them at this point.

After I was released, I dreaded going back to school, and for good reason. My first morning back was nothing but laughs, sneers, and whispers as I walked through the halls. The nasty names I was called before only intensified now. I started to think maybe my plan really was the only way to end this pain. And that's when I saw the twin sisters that I had been so awful to walking my way. I had bullied them so badly up until the day I left, desperately trying to fit in.

"Here we go," I thought. "Now they can make fun of me the way I have them."

As the sisters got closer, I noticed they were carrying something. They stepped up to me, arms outstretched, and handed me a small package and a card. Inside the package was a small potted plant and a candy bar. Inside the card was a handwritten message:

"Kadi, we don't know what you're going through, but we know you can get through it, and we hope you do. We're always here for you. -Amy and Anna"

I once again sobbed, not understanding how someone I had been so awful to could value my life so much.

Let this serve as a reminder.

You never know what battles someone is fighting.

You never know how close they are to giving up.

You never know how much of an impact one moment of love and kindness can have.

Be gentle. Be kind. Be a catalyst for change.

DESTROYING ME

As you're reading this, I'm sure it's difficult to see anything except the pain and destruction, especially if you don't know me on a personal level, which most of you don't. The words I have strung together into sentences, paragraphs, chapters, and eventually, this book are the entirety of what you see. While for me, this book is only a portion of who and what I am, for you, it may be all of me, at least for now.

So, I feel it is necessary to give a disclaimer of sorts. This book is not a tragedy. It's not a story of defeat. Believe me, I understand how ridiculous that sounds. The things I share in this book are, for the most part, not beautiful, happy, or joyous, at least not on their own. But for you to close this book after reading my final word and get all that you can out of it, which I'm praying you do. I have to share the whole picture with you. This includes the dark, depraved, and evil parts.

When you are going through times in your life that seem insurmountable, you feel the full weight of those troubles. There is no sugar coating that pain to yourself. And in those moments, it's so easy to feel as though you don't have what it takes to push through, that you're just not strong enough, that whatever you're facing is far too great, and it's a waste to fight. I remember thinking many times that the healing someone else found wasn't possible for me because I was just up against too much.

THAT is exactly why I have chosen to share my story in such depth. THAT is why I'm such an open book. (Yes, it's okay to laugh at that terrible pun). Although you didn't experience my trauma with me, I need to give you the most detailed picture I can and take you through the darkest parts, down to the very bottom with me, so that when we crawl back up and see the light, you can no longer deny how capable you are of doing it too.

One of my favorite artists, K'naan said in one of his songs, "It is better to light a candle than to curse the dark.[1]" While I know there have been many throughout history who have shared similar thoughts, this one in particular has always stuck with me. If you don't know who he is, you should definitely check him out because WOW, what an inspiration. His story, and this quote specifically, served as a guiding star of sorts.

When everything felt too heavy, instead of giving in to the dark, I would remember that even the tiniest shred of light could guide me. The smallest candle would be enough. And the best part? He said, "It is better to light a candle than to curse the dark." He doesn't say to wait for someone else to light it. He doesn't say that it's impossible to light the candle. He says that I am capable and strong enough, and he speaks from experience.

Kadi and Annika, 2022,
Forever Faithful Photography

So, I need you to remember this as you continue in this book. When things trigger you or it starts to feel heavy, I need you to remember that it has a happy ending. Remind yourself that the beginning and middle don't exist without the end. And how beautiful it is that I am in control of how and when my story ends. Many times, I have felt like what I was battling would be the end of me, but I chose to fight on. The stark contrast between the Kadi you will meet through these

---

1 K'naan. "In the Beginning," The Dusty Foot on the Road Live Album, as written by Brian West Gerald Eaton, Sony/ATV Music Publishing, LLC, Kobalt Music Publishing, Ltd. January 1, 2007.

pages and the Kadi that I am today is remarkable.

This is not a story about my trauma. This is not a story of my defeat. This is not a story where I am a victim. This is not about my abusers.

This is a story of triumph and strength. I am the warrior. I am the queen. I am the victor. I am the main character.

As we continue into my high school years, I want to preface by saying that I will share more of my struggles and journey that I have never spoken about publicly. I have hesitated to share parts of it because I know it may bring judgement. However, I have

Kadi, Freshman year of high school

had a constant recurring thought while writing this book: If I am going to encourage you to speak your truth, even if you do it scared, then I should be doing the same. So, as I write the next few chapters, I will be practicing what I preach and "doing it scared."

Through my freshman and Sophomore years, I did my best to live a "normal" teenage life. I joined the dance team. I made friends. I had everything it took to be a straight-A student, and in the times when I would actually put forth effort and apply myself, I would be. Teachers enjoyed having me as their student, and I followed most of the rules.

However, if you look at me during those years through the lens of knowing I had been sexually abused as a child, the signs are plain as day. I would dress for attention, often wearing heels and mini dresses, as impractical as they were. At the end of my sophomore year, I lost my virginity, and as soon as that relationship ended, I became highly sexually active, and I viewed intercourse as an achievement of sorts. I wanted to see if I could get the popular boys to pay attention to me and would do anything necessary to make that happen.

The more I engaged in these destructive behaviors, the less I valued myself. And the less I valued myself, the more I engaged in these behaviors. I'm sure you're seeing the pattern by now.

I struggled to make meaningful friendships because of my behaviors, and the ones I did make, didn't last.

My junior year would prove to be the height of my destructive behaviors. While I continued on the dance team and doing well in school, I also continued finding my worth completely in male attention. I had given piece after piece of me away to way too many sexual partners. I had devalued myself to what seemed like the lowest I possibly could. And as if that wasn't bad enough, I wasn't even being smart or responsible about the sex I was having, which could only continue on without consequences for so long.

IT COULDN'T BE

March of 2009

We're on a family trip to an all-inclusive resort in Mexico. We spend the days on the beach, and the nights split into groups, exploring all they have to offer. As usual, I had been seeking much older male attention and had found someone interested. So, I would find a way to sneak off to see him at night. I was usually heavily intoxicated and not at all considering any sort of consequences. We had sex multiple times during our time there. I knew no relationship would come from this. He was 24 and lived in Canada. I was 16 and lived in Wyoming. But I didn't care. He was giving me attention, and that felt good.

After we got back home and I went back to school, I started dating a boy in the grade above me. I decided to take it slower this time because I really liked him. We had spent a couple of months together when I started to not feel very well. My best friend at the time went to the store with me to get a pregnancy test. I took it in the bathroom stall before even leaving the store, and it quickly turned positive. This couldn't be. There was no way. I had no had sex with my boyfriend. "It must be something else," I thought. So, I told my Mom, and because I had been honest with her when I lost my virginity, she believed me when I said that my boyfriend and I had not had sex. So, she made me an appointment with my OBGYN and reassured me that it was probably ovarian cysts, giving us a false positive, but not to worry because they had treatments for that.

They gave me a checkup and an ultrasound and told me they would call me with the results. The very next day, I received a call from the doctor. I was indeed pregnant, and when she told me how far along I was, I did the math and realized it was a result of my escapades in

Mexico. Suddenly, a vision of me, drunk as hell and on the bathroom floor of his hotel room, came flooding back, and I remembered clear as day that we had never used a condom or any sort of protection. I was 16 and pregnant, and the dad was a 24-year-old man from Canada. It sounds like something from a soap opera, right?

At that moment, I considered only one option. I was not going to have this baby.

What would the kids at school think of me? What would happen to my spot on the dance team? There was just no way.

Now, I admit that I clearly was not thinking straight, or responsibly, or anything other than a child making a very much adult decision.

The next few weeks consisted of me telling my Mom and Stepdad, and them loving me and supporting me in my decision. Although I found out years later, this was unbelievably hard for them, and they spent a lot of time struggling with what was right and wrong.

We stuck to the story that I had ovarian cysts that had to be removed and made an appointment in CO. It was a multi-day procedure. It required an interview, counseling, and a medical workup. During this interview, I signed paperwork that I did not want to know anything about the baby. I didn't want any details. I was completely disassociated and refused to deal with any of it. I felt very little emotionally during this time and built a wall between myself and everything that was going on. This wall couldn't last forever, though. The guilt, shame, hurt, and everything else that came along with this decision would hit me a few years later.

When we returned home, the rumors were flying, but I did what I could to return to normalcy. I continued on the dance team. I continued my relationship I had begun (I did tell him the truth of everything, and he was very understanding through it all). It wasn't long until summer came, and by the time I returned to school for my senior year, the whispers of "what Kadi did" had mostly disappeared.

Kadi Harnish, Senior Year, 2010

FAKING NORMAL

Looking back on my senior year, it is almost like watching two completely different movies. I was the homecoming princess and president of the community service group "Key Club," and I was heavily involved in the SPAT (Suicide Prevention and Awareness Team) division of our Youth Empowerment Council. I would travel around the state with a wonderful man named Lance, who had lost his son to suicide years earlier, sharing our different yet connected stories of survival. I still practiced and performed with our High-School dance team (although I would end up being injured during a performance that would put me out for our state competition). I had friends. I got good grades. I was taking advanced placement classes and was liked by most of my teachers.

Kadi Senior Photos 2010

On the surface, I looked like a normal, maybe even exceptional teenager. But if you looked past skin deep, or if you asked some of my classmates, I still showed a lot of destructive behaviors and was very much still affected by my trauma. As has been an almost constant theme throughout my young life, I continued to crave and seek out male attention in any form. I had very little self-worth, which fostered and fed into my need for "love." I continued to be sexually unsafe despite the lesson I clearly should have learned just a year ago. I hurt a lot of people by my decisions this year. I made a lot of choices that I later learned deserved apologies.

If I'm being honest, my senior year could have been something truly great. Had I focused more on applying myself and less on winning the "popular boys'" approval through sex, I could have been exceptional. But instead, those exceptional moments were nothing but short glimmers. I was full of potential, thrown away at every turn.

Kadi, graduation day, 2010, with maternal Grandparents

After graduation, I once again didn't live up to my potential. I dreamed of going to college in Boulder, CO, for a double major in public speaking and early childhood education, but I quickly gave up on that idea because I told myself I would never succeed. (Set the bar low so you never miss, right?) Instead, I enrolled in community college and continued to waste my potential. I partied, I continued to hold onto toxic relationships, and I did just enough to barely pass classes.

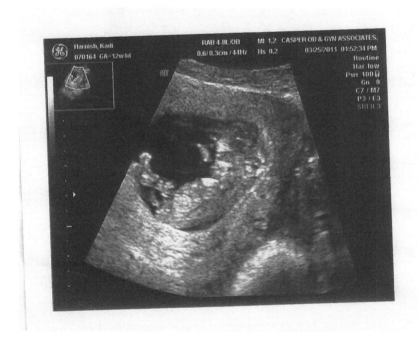

Annika's First Ultrasound, 12 Weeks

Half-way through my freshman year, I found out that I was pregnant by the man I had been dating for four months. We soon found out that I was already 12 weeks pregnant and, therefore, had only been together a month when we conceived. I was 18 years old and scared to death.

I had already accepted the fact that I would more than likely not be able to conceive because, as sadly ironic as it was, my abortion had left blood clots in my uterus that my body refused to pass. They were situated right where a pregnancy was supposed to form, and my doctor had said they would make it incredibly difficult to conceive.

On top of that, I was on birth control pills and took them religiously, not for fear of pregnancy but to help with my unbearable periods.

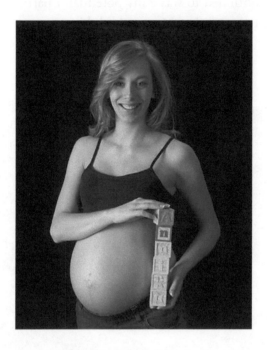

Kadi, 36 weeks along with Annika

You can imagine how overwhelming it was to find out that my entire world was changing. Although I was blessed with an amazing mother and wanted to be just like her, the abuse forced those dreams to fade away. I was so young during the abuse, but I still wondered how on Earth I would protect my future children from those evils if even my mother couldn't protect me. If I couldn't save myself, how would I save someone else? As the abuse had broken me down, I began to accept that being a mother wouldn't be in the cards for me. And here I was, years separated from the abuse but still so damaged. So much of it was repressed that I wasn't yet at a point where I could heal the most damaged pieces of me.

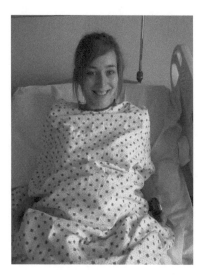

Kadi, Beginning of Labor, 19 years old

This is part of why, in the first few years of my daughter's life, I struggled a great deal. (Being a young mother was an added difficulty) I failed in many ways to set the example that she deserved. As many young parents say, she and I were, in many ways, growing up together. I did the best I could, but I can honestly say that my best then wasn't THE best.

Kadi, 19, with Annika at 3 months

MOTHERHOOD

I still remember the first moment I laid eyes on her. Being 19, gazing at my tiny 6 lb. 3 oz baby, I was so consumed by love but also by fear. Why on earth would God give me a baby? Especially a little girl? What if my daughter was hyper-sexual, even at a young age? What if she tries to kill herself at 13? What if she wastes her talents because she doesn't see them? What will I do if I can't love her enough to save her from this world?

Kadi with Annika, 2 weeks old

I had none of those answers. The only thing I knew was that I had to try. I had to focus on the love that I felt for her, a love that I had never felt before. Through the years together, that love has been

Annika, 6 months old

my guiding light through so many new and unfamiliar darkness, as well as continued battles with some of the same.

There she is. Do you see her swaying joyfully over there? Watch her as she dances in the sunlight. Those ice-blue eyes burn without flames. That almond-brown hair flowed to her waist. Her beaming smile that swallows you whole. She radiates this light that even the sun can't surpass. When you look at her, you know, without a doubt, she's one of a kind. As she spins, a gentle breeze moves her hair out of her face, and time seems to slow for a moment. It's the most beautiful thing you will ever see. She is so perfect, so whole, so entirely 10.

She's beautiful, but there's something extra. There's a fire in her soul. Love for every living thing endlessly pours out of her. She loves unconditionally without even knowing it. She has an endless desire to brighten the lives of those around her. When you are with her, you are enveloped in a joy you've never known before. She will see you wholly: all your fears, shortcomings, and failures, and she will love you the same. She loves in the most pure, whole, and grace-filled way.

If you're one of the lucky ones, you'll know her, and

Kadi, 19, with Annika 6 months

you'll know exactly why she's my wonder-filled girl and my life's greatest accomplishment.

Dear Annika,

As you grow, and it becomes harder for me to shield you from the darkest parts of the world, I pray that you will learn to give yourself the love you so freely give to others. I dream of the day that you will come to realize the immeasurable strength you have inside you and use it as one of your greatest weapons. I hope that you will always remember that boundaries, self-love, and personal accountability are all necessary to be the best human you can be despite society telling you otherwise. When you look at yourself in a mirror, I want you to see the incredible beauty you are. And then I want you to look at your reflection and say, "I am beautiful outside, but I am incomparable in my heart and soul." I yearn for the moments I will get to watch you fearlessly chase your dreams, no matter how daunting and great they may be. This world is not perfect. Humanity has many flaws. There is evil everywhere if you choose to see it, but there is power in choosing to see the light. You are an unmatched source of the purest love, and the day you fully grasp that will be the day the darkness trembles and hides.

Love you to Heaven and back.

Annika, 8 years old, Jessica Simkin Photography

MY GREATEST CHALLENGE

The beginning of what would be my greatest challenge as a mother started when she was three. We were living in Alabama for a short time for a work contract when I received a call from my mother, which seemed completely unimportant at the time.

"Hi, Mom."

"Hi, Sweetie. How are you doing? I miss you."

"I miss you too. Hopefully, we'll be able to come back and visit for Annie's birthday."

"That would be great. You know you're always welcome to stay here. Just let us know."

"Thank you. I will. Is everything okay? Something doesn't feel right."

"I'm okay, sweetie. I just wanted to let you know that I got a phone call from the Sheriffs in (the town we lived in). They will be calling you to ask some questions about (Astaroth)."

"Oh. Okay. Why? This seems kind of out of nowhere. It's been like nine years since we've seen him."

"Well, I don't want to say too much, but there were a couple of other girls who were close to him when they were younger that came forward and said he was hurting them. So, the Sheriffs want to see if you had any similar experiences or any information or anything. I already told them everything I know. Don't worry, sweetie. You're not in trouble or anything. Just be honest with them and answer their questions the best you can."

"Okay. I won't be much help. But I'll do my best. Thank you for letting me know. I love you."

"I love you too. I'll call you tomorrow, okay?"

"Okay. Talk to you tomorrow. Bye."

"Bye, sweetie."

The next day, my phone rang, and when I looked at the Caller ID, I knew it was them.

They asked me about our history with Astaroth, how long he was in our lives, etc. It seemed like they were just gathering background information. Then they started asking if he had ever abused me, specifically sexually. (Now, here is the part where it gets messy.) I said no.

Kadi- "Get Loud" Photoshoot, Phoenix Photos Photography, 2017

Everything had been completely repressed. So, while I know now that the answer should have been yes, my honest answer at the time was NO. They then explained to me that two other young women had come forward. He had held a very similar position in their lives, making himself a "part of their family," and had abused them for years while they were young. They had both come forward after turning 18 and because the abuse was from years prior, they were trying to build a stronger case against him by locating more victims. It was clearly a pattern for Astaroth, so they knew these weren't the only two. I explained to them that while I could testify to some instances of physical abuse and be a character witness, I didn't recall any sexual abuse, so I would be no help there.

(I would later find out that these girls were so afraid that they wouldn't be able to prosecute him without more victims that they decided not to testify, and the case was dropped. If either of you is reading this, I am so sorry that I couldn't stand by your side in the way you needed. I hope and pray you have found the same healing I have and are thriving in every way.)

The Sheriffs thanked me and ended the phone call, and I thought that was the end of it. But I was horribly mistaken. For the next three years, I began to have night terrors, where I would wake up silently screaming and unable to breathe. At first, it was only every once in a while. But as time progressed, they would come more and more often, eventually being an almost nightly thing. These night terrors didn't make sense to me though. The way I felt was as if I was being murdered. Everything was so vivid and so real and so visceral. But the dreams themselves seemed to be nothing more than the pattern of the back seat of a truck, the walls of a business Astaroth used to own, or the bridge that ran over the railroad tracks from my childhood. The things I saw seemed so nothing, but the way they made me feel was inexplainable.

Along with the nightmares, I was showing visible signs of trauma. I was having panic attacks triggered by the sound of the swings in the park by our house and other seemingly innocent things. I was slowly beginning a downward spiral at this point. But just enough for the people closest to me to notice. I struggled to eat or sleep. I disconnected and disassociated. I was losing weight. And my depression and anxiety were at an all-time high. I had no idea what any of it meant, but I knew it wasn't right, and I knew it meant something.

So, when my daughter was 6, I decided to revisit the place I called home as a child, hoping to understand what these dreams meant. It's actually ironic. I had no expectations. But at the same time, I somehow knew I needed to do this. So, I asked one of my closest childhood friends to meet up for a day, and I made the 3-hour drive back to "hell" for the first time.

THE RETURN

She drove me around to all of our favorite spots as kids: the park with the froggy slide that we would walk to from my house, the pizza place across the street from our elementary school, the bowling alley, and "Oasis," where we spent all summer. I shared with her why I was interested in revisiting these spots, and she asked if I wanted to go back to any of the places from my dreams. I had not found the answers I was searching for yet, so I said okay.

We drove to every spot we could think of: my old house, the old business, even the bridge. We talked about everything we remembered from our childhood and searched for any answers that may have been out there. We did everything we could think of until it was time for me to drive home, and as I left, I was honestly disappointed. I was no closer to the answers now than when I had made this drive this morning. Nothing had happened. I had gained no understanding or guidance. Aside from seeing my old friend, I had gained not a single thing. I made the entire drive home silent, empty, and more confused than ever.

Although I had not gained any understanding on this trip, the nightmares and panic attacks continued with no reprieve. They even began intensifying. Just a month or so after returning home, it all started to cave in around me. I began to unlock my most traumatic memories, and the moments that I had worked so hard to repress began flooding back. I experienced a level of fear and anxiety I had never known before. I began to understand that I wasn't "hyper-sexual." I was groomed, manipulated, and abused. I finally understood that my idea of worth being directly related to sexuality was twisted, warped, and incorrect. I realized that the weight of the guilt and pain that had pushed me to self-harm and suicidal thoughts was not mine to carry.

Once these floodgates opened, there was no stopping all that would crash in.

MY FIRST FLASHBACK

Everything is louder when it's silent.

Your heartbeat.

His grunts.

You can taste his sweat. He can taste your fear.

His hands are ice. But not because they're cold. Every time they touch you, they feel like they slice through your flesh. Every bruise is a stab wound you're sure will never heal.

You struggle to breathe, unsure if it's the weight of his body crushing yours or the realization that nothing will ever be the same.

The rhythm of his movements is the most sickening song you've ever heard.

Over and over. Beat after beat.

No sound, and yet it roars so loudly that it shakes you.

Boom.

Thud.

Boom.

You wish your heart would stop beating so this could end.

He's dancing away with your soul.

You want to say no again. But it only makes him happy. Your first 100 pleas for him to stop didn't mean anything. Why would one more save you?

Down, down, down. You shove your conscious awareness to the darkest depths. The way he brushes the hair out of your face so he can see your tears. His smell of smoke and musty soil.

"This is what good girls do." He's winded when he speaks.

Numb.

Down. Down. Down. Hide it away. Make yourself numb.

You're sure it's almost over.

But the worst has only started.

It's pointless to hold someone down when they have nothing left to fight with. It's a waste of time to cover someone's mouth when their throat is too dry to scream. But he does it anyway.

Time stops in those last two minutes. It seems like years pass, years of your childhood, innocence, and joy. All fade away like dust in the cold, damp air.

Ten minutes. A lifetime of agony.

You close your eyes hard enough to cause flickers of colors. One last thrust. It should be over now.

It's never over, then.

What comes after is what breaks your soul.

"I love you," he whispers, out of breath. "Now clean yourself up."

You've avoided looking this entire time. You can't stand to see what he's done to you. But you have to face it because if you get blood on the seat of his truck, there will be hell to pay.

A thief. He's a Thief of joy. Thief of innocence. Thief of your peace and soul for years to come.

PEAK

Oh, sweet girl. If only I could hold you and promise you that it will be okay. I would show you that this will end. First, the physical pain. Then, the spiritual damage. I know you're broken. You're bruised. You feel like you have nothing left. I will not lie and tell you that those feelings will pass without a fight. I won't make you empty promises about how everything will be okay because it won't.

Not for a long time.

This will be the hardest battle of your life. Hatred will try to consume you. For him. And yourself. Thoughts of being damaged, worthless, and disgusting will become your normal, and forgiveness and self-love will feel so far out of reach. Please believe that you have what it takes.

It's ironic, isn't it? It will take years of your blood, sweat, and tears to forget the taste of his.

Fight on, baby girl. Gods got you.

THE TIME SINCE

In the years since my first, what I would call full flashback, I have worked endlessly in many ways to heal the broken pieces inside of me so that I can break this generational cycle and give her a chance at being whole. As I write this, we have made it just a couple of months shy of 12 years old. And although I haven't been anywhere near perfect as a mom, she is EXACTLY a couple of months shy of turning 12.

She's not 13, not 16, not 20. She blushes in embarrassment at the thought of kissing someone, and her idea of a "boyfriend" is what most would call a best friend and doesn't come with any strings attached. She will be the first girl on my maternal side, for at least the last four generations, who made it to 12 years old without being sexually abused. I know our battle is not over yet. I am not done healing myself and protecting her. But wow, what an incredible victory.

It has not been easy. I have struggled and fallen more times than I can count. I have walked a thousand miles through the depths of the greatest desperation only to fall at the very last second and have to start over. I have tried everything anyone ever recommended to heal: self-help books, seminars, retreats, groups, church, therapy, pharmaceuticals, crystals, homeopathic remedies, lucid dreaming.... You name it, I've tried it. While there absolutely is no

Annika, 11 years old,
first day of 6th grade

magic fix for all I've been through, there are a few specific things I credit for being pivotal in my growth.

1. CHURCH.

While I know church and religion can be very touchy subjects, I feel it's important that I acknowledge the role they played. During about three of the most difficult years of my healing, I was fully immersed in a local church. I went to service every Sunday, a women's group every Friday afternoon, and a small group bible study every week as well. I built beautiful relationships with many of the congregation. Many of them listened to me and supported me while I shared the darkest details as they unfolded. The church gave me food, furniture, and even a place to stay when my life began to crumble around me. I called one of the pastors at midnight, desperate for someone to help me, and he talked me down from taking my life and then connected me with the support I needed after. These people saw me as I was: broken, bloodied, and the very definition of a sinner. They met me in my mess and expected nothing of me. They loved me the way Jesus calls us to love, and he used them to save my life.

2. EMDR THERAPY

I tried years and years of therapy, both as a child and an adult. I never viewed it as a waste of time, but I really struggled to see what all the hype was about. It, most often, felt like it didn't really make a difference for me. And that is why I almost didn't give EMDR therapy a chance. But, after my trip unlocked all of the repressed trauma, I was desperate for any relief. EMDR was different than all my previous therapy. Instead of sharing about whatever was on my mind that day or examining things that had happened that week, I was facing my trauma head-on. I was choosing to go back and relive those memories that caused me so much pain, but this time with a secret weapon. I would hold rods in my hand that would vibrate when signaled. They served as my connection to the present. I would guide my therapist back through my abuse, step by step, with as much detail as possible. I know what you're thinking. Yes, it was agonizing. Yes, I wanted to quit. Yes, I questioned the validity of all of it. But I trusted the process. And as I would take him back through those flashbacks, he would send the signal to the rods in my hands to vibrate, to keep me tethered to reality. It was a long, difficult process, but I was able to, one trauma at a time, reprogram my brain to understand that I was no longer living in those situations, that I was safe now, and that I didn't have to live in a constant state of "fight or flight" anymore. I slowly took my power back from the flashbacks and, therefore, began to take my power back from my abusers.

3. A SUPPORT SYSTEM

I know this one seems cheesy and cliché, but just trust that it's more important than I can say. When you have lived through traumas such as mine, they often manifest in addictions and other destructive behaviors. You make terrible decisions and hurt the people who love you. Those things don't stop suddenly just because you decide to heal. Honestly, for me, it probably got worse before it got better. I had to touch every fiber of my past. I had to sit with it and allow it to rip me to shreds again before I learned how to repair myself. During those times, I was blessed with a few friends and family who saw the real me and loved me, even when I was unlovable. They gave me grace during my worst moments and supported me, even in moments where I don't know if I would have had the strength to do the same for them. They saw me fighting every day and taking steps to heal, and that was enough for them to continue to cheer me on. I honestly wouldn't be where I am today without them.

*Dave (Kadi's Biological Dad) and Randy
(Kadi's step-dad) 2021, family camping trip*

HEALING

Every day, I walk further and further into my healing. And every day, I learn more and more about myself, my trauma, and my life. This book is ultimately meant to serve as a guide of sorts. It's not a map because my steps won't be the exact same as any other survivors' steps, but hopefully, they will inspire other survivors even to TRY to heal because that decision happens to be the scariest part.

I want the very last part of this book to be the bits and pieces of lessons that I have learned over the last few years. They are choppy and seemingly random. I have written them at different points through the

last few years, focusing more on raw, honest thoughts than how "cohesive" they would be in this book. So, bear with me because they are not as polished as most of my other writing. But they don't need to be pretty to give you something to grasp onto as a starting point in your journey to all you deserve. And with that, we begin the most magnificent PEAK of the entire book.

Kadi and fiancé Matt, engagement photos, 2023, Jessica Simkin Photography

EVERYTHING IS LOUDER
WHEN IT'S SILENT

Dear Kadi, precious, precious girl,

It's been 18 years since the last time they hurt you. So much has changed. I'm sorry that you have been hidden away for so long. You're safe to come out now. There is so much I want to tell you now that we're finally free.

I know you used to wonder how you would ever be able to be a good mother. I know you thought that you were far too broken to love, protect, and guide any children you may have. Well, guess what? You have a beautiful, kind, and WHOLE little girl. She is almost 12 now, and you have protected her so fiercely. She still blushes at the thought of even holding hands with a boy, and her innocence still belongs to her. No one has taken any pieces of her that are not theirs to take. She is encouraged endlessly by you. She is loved unconditionally by you. She is given a space that is constant and calm enough to be honest and open with you. Although she wasn't planned, you have pushed so hard to become the greatest mother you can be. You have given her everything you never thought you would be able to and then some. You should be so proud of yourself.

I remember the nights you used to lie awake crying because you didn't understand what love was. It wasn't supposed to hurt, but the "love" you were given hurt very much. It may have taken us a long time, but we finally found the love we dreamed of before our fairy-tales were replaced with nightmares. We now have a love that is so safe. It has become the rock that holds us up through any of life's struggles. We have found a man who doesn't hurt us, a man who doesn't manipulate or use us. His words aren't boulders used to crush us. His hands aren't chains, used to hold us down while he takes what isn't his. His "I love you really does mean "I love you." We are a gift in his life, and he reminds us of that daily. He is constant. He is strong. He is fierce in his love for us. He knows what we have been through, and he loves us even more because of how hard we have fought to overcome it. He is so proud of us. He has shown us what love always should have been. You're going to love him. He is everything we have dreamed of and more.

I look back and I can still feel the fear that grips you by the throat. Your silence is deafening. You can't tell anyone what he has done to you. You have to protect those you love by keeping this secret. You will forever be suffocated by these evils that haunt you. If you try to speak up, no one will believe you. And he will only hurt you more. He has threatened you countless times. Every time his hands touched you, he reminded you that there was no one to save you and looking for help would only make him angry. He calls you weak and worthless. But he is so wrong. Not only do you find the courage to speak up to save yourself, but you now scream your story from the rooftops to save others. You now speak on stages in front of hundreds (and someday thousands of survivors). Now, you are sharing your hope and strength on the pages of your book that will be a best-seller (I just know it). You did everything he said you'd never do, and you became everything he said you'd never be. You are a beacon of light for those who are suffering, and you are silenced no longer.

I see the hurt in your eyes. I know your soul feels as battered, bloodied, and bruised as your body shows. Every time he violates you, your soul cracks again. Every time he steals your innocence, he rips away another piece, and you are even less whole. It's true. Those pieces are valuable beyond measure. He has shattered you into thousands of fragments and cast you aside as trash. It seems impossible to put your pieces back together with any semblance of beauty. But against all odds, we do it. We are more whole now than we've ever been, and I need you to know that that's because of your strength. Your steadfast courage carried us through the darkest years and brought us to a place where I could fill our fractures with gold. We are stronger than we ever were. We are brighter than we ever were. And we are far more beautiful than either of us could have imagined. The pieces he stole have been replaced. The havoc he wreaked has been undone. The war has been won.

I need you to hear me now.

I love you. I love you. I love you. I know there have been many years where I haven't shown you the love you deserve, but your worth has never changed. You are and have always been far more precious than can be put into words. I'm sorry for the years I spent treating you as broken, worthless, and damaged. I'm sorry for the times I sliced your skin and the plans I made to end our life. I'm sorry for the alcohol I consumed to try and drown the memories. I'm sorry you had to hide in the shadows for so long before I was strong enough for you to come out. You deserved to be protected. You deserved to be loved. You deserved a childhood as it was meant to be. As much as I wish I could change all of that for you, we both know I cannot. But I have worked endlessly to give us the safety, security, and love we always deserved. There is so much beauty in the life I have created for us now. I promise you will never be made to feel dirty, broken, or less than worthy again.

Your Trauma is not all that exists.

HAPPY?

Being asked to share a happy, positive memory from before my abuse was a seemingly impossible task until I accepted that I was more than my abuse and, therefore, my past was more than my abuse as well. What is a happy, positive, innocent memory you have from before all the abuse began?

This was a tough question for me because my abuse began so young. I can recall countless memories and definitively say they were during or after the time of my abuse, but It's hard for me to recall a memory from my early childhood and definitively say it was before my abuse began. However, I have a lot of fond memories from the years of my abuse.

There were parts of my early life that felt almost untouched by the abuse, like a gasp of air when you're drowning. They were maybe even more sweet because I knew what the other side felt like.

I found joy in the moments where I felt safe, no matter how simple they were: hunting for grasshoppers in the yard, helping my Grandmother with her crosswords while we shared a Caramello bar, my mother reading baby Disney books to me, my Dad and I waiting patiently for my overpriced sailor hat with "Kadi" spray painted on the front at the county fair.

Looking back now, I can see that the loving, positive, happy memories far outweigh the memories of abuse in number. But the memories of abuse were and sometimes still are a much, much heavier weight to carry. The abuse seeped into every nook and cranny of my life, which took away any "black and white" in my life and made everything "grey." Having to piece a lot of my childhood together through repressed memories makes it even more difficult to mark a point that was "before the abuse." Most of the time, I feel like I am refurbishing a stained-glass window that was shattered again and again over many years with no reference to how it should look when it's finished.

"Was this piece here when it was first built?"

"What was this part intended to look like?"

"Which break caused this specific fissure?"

Kadi and Kathi (mom) after Kadi danced at NBA Halftime 2010

I can see the beauty of it when I look at it in its entirety and focus on the bigger picture instead of each break and blemish. Despite those parts, I can see the pieces that are still whole, protected by those experiences of love, joy, and safety that existed in the same world as the experiences of abuse. My PTSD wants me to believe that a childhood of abuse and a childhood of joy are mutually exclusive, that I can only choose one, and that choice was made for me. But through the work I have done to heal, I have learned that I am allowed to have both.

I had abusers.

But I also had a mother, father, and brothers who loved me dearly.

I was a victim of unspeakable acts of abuse.

But I also was a funny, sweet, beautiful little girl.

I was given many awful memories.

But I was also given many memories of love that I treasure.

There may not be years of my life "before Astaroth" that I can reflect on to find solace when my trauma feels heavy. But I have chosen to find those moments in the years "during Astaroth," and he will never take that away from me.

BABY STEPS

Sometimes, when I feel as if I've hit a wall and I don't know how on earth I'm going to muster up the strength to climb over it when everything feels heavy, and I can barely breathe, let alone fight, those are the moments when I crave simplicity. Reading a self-help book feels like it would take too much time, time that I don't have. Thinking about attending a self-help workshop can feel so uncomfortable and unachievable. Going to therapy may even feel like "too much" sometimes. I may not even have the strength to reach out for help because then I will have to explain how and why I'm triggered, and that's exhausting and requires me to be vulnerable in a moment I might not be able to. Now, don't get me wrong, these are all things I love and use, obviously, because you're reading my self-help book right now. I talk about therapy and workshops and all of the wonderful coping tools I use. But what about the moments when I have next to nothing left? What about when I am exhausted, defeated, and feel frozen? Do you know that feeling? When you have to fight even to crawl? Forget about walking or running, right? What do I do then?

This is where some of the advice I was given as a child but never fully understood until adulthood comes in.

"Baby steps, Kadi."

I remember looking at my Dad, my Mom, my Stepdad, my Stepmom, my teachers, and pretty much every adult in my life in complete confusion and probably a little judgement too. And then I would think, "I'm not a baby. I know how to walk. Thanks for nothing," as I would walk away. Then, it was usually about something along the lines of how to clean my room or how to cope with my 5th grade best friend making a newer "bester" friend. The problems I was seeking advice on were small, but the advice I was given was

71

momentous. And maybe that's why it didn't fully sink in until many, many years later.

Now, I know I was given this advice during the years between those childhood memories and adulthood, but I must've brushed it off all those times the same way I did back then because I can't recall any of those times in between. However, I vividly remember the day it all finally clicked for me.

I was halfway through my shift at work. At the time, I was a heavy equipment operator in one of North America's largest coal mines. My repressed memories had only recently started to surface, and I was essentially clueless about how to navigate the flashbacks and all that came with them. I was having a pretty normal, monotonous day. It was just me in my giant dump truck, picking up a load of topsoil at point A and dumping it at point B. Round and round, over and over.

Next thing I know, I'm shaking, I'm crying, and I'm gasping for full breath. I suddenly feel like I'm in a different place, and a different time, and somehow, a different me. I'm in his truck again. How? I'm not this little girl anymore. I'm 25 years old. I know I am. I must be hallucinating. But I can feel the breeze coming in the window. I can smell the wet grass and trees outside. I can hear the radio so clearly that I could sing along. I feel sick. This seems so real, but it can't be. My tiny hands are covered in sweat. It's not hot. I'm just so scared. Why am I scared? I don't understand any of this.

I continued to exist in this almost parallel universe for what felt like both an entire lifetime and a singular moment. I watched a man that I loved and admired and thought I could trust hurt me in ways I could not explain. I was me now, watching me then. But I was also me then, living this nightmare and begging me now for help. It's impossible to explain fully, but if you've experienced it, there's no mistaking it. I was somehow reliving a memory I never knew existed.

When I came to, my truck was stopped in the parking ditch, and I was sitting on the ground underneath it, my back completely supported by its giant tire. I had just experienced what I now know was my first flashback of the abuse. I was completely exhausted. I couldn't think straight, I could hardly breathe, and I honest to God felt like I could not and would not survive. I was completely consumed by anger, pain, and confusion. I didn't know where to turn or what to do.

This was one of those moments where I desperately needed something more. There was no way I could call anyone and explain what had just happened, and I definitely wasn't in a place to crack open a book on "flashbacks for dummies."

I leaned forward and fell onto my knees. I turned my head towards the sky and begged for a way forward, for an answer. I was in survival mode and needed a way out.

I stood up, my legs trembling. In fear or out of weakness? Maybe

Kadi, 22 and Annie, 3, 2014

both. My brain sent the signal to step forward, but I was frozen. A step forward meant I wasn't giving up, and therefore, I had to fight. But the fight would require a strength far greater than I had, so how could I even fathom taking that step? And then, I heard all of the voices from before crying out in unison, "Baby steps, Kadi." It was as if that little Kadi I had just failed to save was somehow reaching out to me, pointing me to the only beacon of light that existed in this new, dark, cold world.

Since that day, anytime I face something that feels impossible to get through, I do my best to remind myself that I don't have to do anything fantastic, huge, or incredible to do something good enough. I only have to be brave enough to take baby steps. One baby step after another will still get me to the end goal as long as I don't quit.

Is depression kicking my ass? Baby steps.

Are flashbacks and nightmares ramping up? Baby steps.

Struggling with self-worth again? Baby steps.

Even today, as I'm writing this, it has taken 6 hours, two changes of location, and a lot of grace to get less than two pages done. But you know what? That's okay because these pages are just another baby step.

You don't always need anything extravagant or out of reach to be okay. Maybe, for right now, you need to be told that whatever you have to give is enough, and even a baby step is a step.

WORDS ARE POWERFUL.

There are pieces of the abuse that still linger with me, pieces that have faded very little over decades. I have often wondered if they will ever evanesce. The blood has washed away. The tears have dried. The bruises have healed. But the words, the words live on. Their grasp remains firm.

"I didn't break you. You were broken before I found you."

"No one will ever love you."

"Stop that. It's not okay to cry".

"I'm a good man. No one will ever believe you."

"If you tell anyone anything, I will kill you and your Mom, that you love so much."

"You might be worth something if you weren't so disgusting."

"This is all you're good for. It's a shame you're not very good at it."

"I always get what I want when I want it, and for now, that's you."

"If you know what's good for you, you'll stay quiet until I'm done."

"If you love me, you'll do this."

"It only hurts the first time."

"You'll learn to like it. Eventually, you'll even want it".

"The man who gets you someday will thank me for teaching you."

"This is what you were meant for."

"God put you in my life for me to use. My happiness is your happiness."

"This is what good girls do."

These were far more than words. They were intentional. They were perception. They were an expectation. They were a retelling of all I was and a foretelling of all I would ever be. They were the entirety of who I was through his eyes, and they found a home deep inside of me.

75

RELENTLESS

Now, which came first, the chicken or the egg? Would I prove him right because of the damage he caused me? Or was he right because I was already damaged? Did he take a perfect, innocent little girl and mold her into his perfect victim? Or did he simply get lucky, with his perfect victim falling into his lap?

That was probably one of the most difficult questions I grappled with. I felt as though I needed the answer, but this wasn't an answer I had. I knew that in order to move forward, I would have to rewrite these words. But how would that be possible when they occupied an ever-present place in my life? They were my shadow, existing obscurely in every thought and every action.

He was long gone, and I was still living as if these words were being recited to me daily.

I continued to seek male attention, often from much older, much more broken men. I continued to stay silent. I continued to place my worth solely in what I had to offer sexually to someone, anyone else. I continued to give pieces of me away as if I weren't already completely void. I gave and gave and gave and gave, every time, breathing life into the words he uttered to me and about me so many years ago. It was a self-fulfilling prophecy, and I was powerless to stop it... until I wasn't.

When you are having a conversation in public, but your words keep getting overpowered by the noises and sounds around you, what do you do?

Exactly.

You raise your voice.

So that's what I did when I couldn't seem to quiet him; I would just be louder. Every time I recognized his words replaying through my actions or thoughts, I would turn my volume up.

"I am worthy. I'm not broken. I am more than what has been done to me. I am valuable beyond measure. I will continue to survive ALL of this. I am enough. I am meant for more."

At first, it was completely a "fake it 'til you make it" approach. I didn't fully believe any of what I was saying. If I'm being completely honest, I still believed the words he had told me, but I couldn't let them know that. I had to drown them out until they became weak and existed mostly in the background, and then, I had to turn my volume up once again. I could not afford for any voice other than mine to be the loudest, and I could not afford for my voice to agree with his at all.

What started as a shaking, trembling, altogether forced voice became a fight song, shouted from the rooftops without hesitation or fear.

Words are powerful. They are never merely written or spoken. They are embedded in the hearts and souls of those whose eyes and ears they touch. They will hide away and outlast all physical reminders of their first existence.

They are either disregarded or strengthened.

There is no in-between.

So, be mindful of the words you heed and the voices you feed.

Remember that no one's words will ever be truer than the ones you choose to speak.

Pay attention to the dialogue lurking in the shadows.

And understand that it's all going to be a jumbled mess for a while, at least until you find your volume.

It's okay if things don't make sense right now.

One of the hardest things for me to come to terms with over the years is that my trauma and my healing have been so messy. They do not look like the examples you see in the movies. They have gone against everything I would have ever thought had I been on the outside looking in. Honestly, if I hadn't experienced it for myself, someone telling me that they had "forgotten" years of sexual abuse would sound like absolute bullshit. It seems so unlikely, and so made up, and so just... fake. I acknowledge that a large part of that may be the fact that I was told "no one will believe you" so many times that I even struggled to believe myself. Even so, that is probably the one single thing I spent the most time grappling with. I asked my therapist. I did my own research. I talked to other survivors. Every direction I looked was telling me that it was wholly possible and actually quite common, and yet, I continued to silence myself. For years, I spoke about all of this only in confidential rooms. I only saw the repression as a burden. I hadn't found the strength yet to see how beautiful and effective it truly was.

Even while I was learning to accept that what my brain had done was truly possible, no matter how impossible it seemed, I learned a lot about my flashbacks and the way they happened. I was spending so much time trying to prove myself wrong that, by default, I gained an unmatched clarity and understanding of this new part of me. What I had not understood in the slightest, I now knew to its deepest parts. There was no denying that my flashbacks were very much real in the moment and very much based in reality from my past.

Naturally, other people have been curious about this phenomenon as well. I have often been asked what it's like to have a flashback after my trauma has been repressed for so long.

For years, I couldn't describe it as anything other than suffocating, deafening, overwhelming. There were no words to express what would happen accurately. I didn't know my triggers. I didn't understand exactly what was happening, and it would instantly snap me into fight or flight mode, which made it impossible to think about anything other than just surviving. One second, everything felt "normal," and the next, I would be in a crumpled ball on the floor, sobbing uncontrollably, shaking in fear.

I will never forget the first time a flashback hit me full force. I was standing in my bedroom, windows open, curtains drawn. The sunshine was pouring in, along with the sound of happy birds chirping. The sound of children playing at the park sang through my windows. Everything was peaceful, joyous even, until it wasn't. Suddenly, I was transported into a damp, cold room. It was familiar, but it was like I had seen it in a movie, not like I had been there myself. I was watching a little girl be violated by a grown man. I couldn't stop it. They couldn't see me. I could feel her pain, but I was as helpless as her. I knew her somehow; I knew I did, but I wasn't her. That just wasn't possible.

I searched for anything to focus on, anything other than her. Sights, smells, tastes, anything. And then, there it was, the sound of metal creaking as it moved. Almost melodically, creak, creak, creak.

I opened my eyes, swollen from the tears. I gasped for air as if I had been drowning. I was home, back in the sunshine, back in reality. But that sound was still there. I knew that sound, not only from the hoses I had heard only moments ago, turning in whatever hell I was in but also from the sound of summer. It was the sound of the chains on the park swing set as children pumped their legs back and forth. That was it. That sound was what set everything off.

There have been many triggers since then, and I'm sure there will be many more. Recognizing them and understanding where they come from has been a huge step in gaining control of my life again. I have searched for answers as to why they happen and how to prevent them, how to "shut down" that part of my subconscious. I wanted so badly to make them go away completely. While that hasn't happened (and I don't know if it ever truly will), I have discovered a lot about my flashbacks and myself in relation to them. I hope that by sharing my experience and the progress I've made, I can aid others in their battle against their trauma.

If I had to draw you a picture of how and why a flashback is triggered, this is what it would be.

There are two old film reels playing simultaneously. One is now, the everyday moments of my present. It is every second of my current life, playing in exact time with what I'm experiencing.

The other is all of my repressed memories, on repeat, showing every second, down to the smallest detail. Every sound, every smell, every taste, every touch.

I can't watch either reel at will. They play unnoticed in the background until a moment on one aligns perfectly with a moment on the other. Maybe a smell from one matches a smell from the other or a sight from one matches a sight from the other. In this case, it was the sound of swings moving that matched the sound of high-pressure water hoses turning as they were being used. The second that two completely separate moments match up, the reels stop playing separately and almost join for a short time. Neither my present nor my past exist on their own. I am living physically in my present, but emotionally, spiritually, and mentally, I am reliving my past.

Now, imagine the reels flashing on their screens independently. The reel of my present continues moving without interruption as the reel of my repressed memories plays over and over on repeat. Most of the time, they don't line up. Rarely does the exact moment of that sound from my subconscious hit its screen as the same exact moment I can hear the squeak of the park swings. This is part of why my flashbacks are so random and unexpected.

Another reason I believe they are so random is because of the way my subconscious shares them with my conscious mind. It hid these away originally to protect me the best way it knew how. I was a child who could not process what was being done to me, so my subconscious made a choice to push them so far down that I wouldn't have to face them until I had a better chance of surviving them. It's almost as if my subconscious pushed all of my trauma back and then built a dam to keep it there. The pressure increased with every new trauma thrown at me. The dam was effective for years until I was informed that Astaroth had been accused of abuse by other young girls. This created the smallest hairline fracture on that dam. Not big enough for the naked eye to detect but not small enough to keep moments of these memories from seeping through. The pattern of the fabric I now know was the backseat of his truck, the tree by the railroad tracks I now know was one of his favorite places to take me, all of these small glimpses into moments that had been hidden away. As more of these came through, I knew something was missing. Why would I think of that fabric so often, feeling sick every time I remembered the way it smelled but not be able to recall anything else? That is why I decided to revisit the place where most of this abuse occurred. I was hoping just to gain understanding, not realizing that this could cause that fracture to burst suddenly and all of the pain, trauma, and abuse to flood my current life and leave me gasping for air.

It's funny to speak of my subconscious as if it's a being completely separate from me. I know that it's not. I fully understand that my subconscious exists in the same space that my conscious does. But my subconscious can access so much that my conscious cannot and can control what my conscious cannot. In some ways, it was the hero that has saved me time and time again throughout my life.

When these flashbacks began happening, it was very difficult for me to live a normal life. I struggled to process the trauma and accept all that had happened to me. This is why I believe my subconscious built a barrier, yet again, to protect me. Each time I have a flashback of the same memory, it gives me another small piece of the puzzle because the whole thing at once

Kadi and Biological Dad on a camping trip, 2021

would absolutely break me. So, it allows me to have small parts of any one memory each time I have a flashback, processing it and then piecing it together with the others. Once I have the entirety of that specific memory, I can heal enough to take my control back, and it no longer haunts me the way that it used to. One by one, I have pieced together trauma after trauma from my childhood, fought like hell to heal from it, and then set it aside, continuing the battle the next day with the next trauma.

I often wonder if there is an endless supply of repressed memories that will continue for the rest of my life, and I've had to come to terms with the fact that I will probably never know. This may be just another part of the war I will be fighting for the rest of my life, even if I win the battle every day. This used to scare me and make me want to give up. Why on earth would I want to do this for the rest of my life? I am beaten down, bruised, and exhausted. If there is no end, there is no victory, right?

Wrong.

There is victory in every day I get up. There is victory in every smile. There is victory in every cycle I break. There is victory in every healthy relationship I nurture. There is victory in every bad habit I break. There is victory in every day I choose to keep fighting so I can continue to learn and love. There is so much victory in every moment of my life, but the greatest victory is in every one of you who finds strength in my story.

5 TRUTHS

I often get asked what advice I would give to other survivors, and in those moments, I freeze up. I malfunction, and the only thing I can think of is "Error. Error." How could I possibly compress years of trauma and years of healing into a passing conversation? How can I know that the select few pieces of advice I choose to share in these moments are the exact pieces that a person needs to hear? How can I have the biggest impact with the time they have given me? My goal is that every person who asks me this question walks away feeling empowered and encouraged by at least one piece of advice I've shared. So, over the years that I have spent growing and healing, I have focused a lot of time on the way I answer this.

If I could share any 5 truths with another survivor, this is what they would be:

1) HEALING HURTS.

There is no part of healing that doesn't come with its own kind of pain. The traumas that you are battling began a cycle of pain. The flashbacks, nightmares, depression, anxiety, triggers, and unhealthy coping mechanisms you have developed to survive are all part of this constant cycle of hurt you were thrust into. I know it's heavy. I know it feels never-ending. I know it seems completely cliché to say, "It's going to get worse before it gets better."

But I also know there is truth to that. So, when you're done laughing at that, hear me say this: If you want to heal the deepest depths of your soul, if you wish for freedom from the grasp that your trauma has on you, if you are truly ready to get down to the nitty-gritty of this

83

cycle, then you have to stand firm. You must feel the anger, resentment, pain, and loss that others have forced on you and acknowledge that it has a place in your journey. Before you can leave the pain behind, you are going to have to sit with it. It's going to hurt like hell, and you have to know that's okay.

2) HEALING ISN'T PASSIVE.

It isn't magic. It doesn't exist within a singular moment. There will never be a morning when you wake up and you are rescued from your trauma. There is no knight in shining armor that will slay the dragon and whisk you away from your misery once and for all. When you have had to fight through the unbelievable abuses that we have, every day will be a new dragon guarding yet another locked tower. You will have to be your own hero and choose daily to overcome whatever beasts may stand in your way. Today, your battle may be to show up honestly in therapy. Tomorrow, it may be choosing healthy coping methods after flashbacks and nightmares. No matter which part of your trauma you face that day, no matter how exhausted you are after the war that raged inside you, I hope you continue to stand on the frontline day after day. I believe you have the strength to come out on top through every struggle, and I hope you choose to do just that.

3) HEALING ISN'T LINEAR.

Your journey isn't going to be a straight shot from the darkness you feel today to the freedom you can experience tomorrow. When you show up daily for yourself, you will experience incredible progress. But that progress will often be followed by more struggles. You know the old saying, "Two steps forward, one step back." Yeah, I know, another cliché. But there's a reason they have stuck around all this time. The truth to this one is hard to hear and even harder to accept. Without setbacks, there would be no growth. The reality of life is that there will always be challenges, just as sure as the sun will always set to rise again the next day. However, these hard times aren't guaranteed to hold you back. The way you understand them and view them is what determines if they are a stopping point or a stepping stone. Once you recognize that your healing journey is an overall picture instead of small snapshots of the difficult times, you take the power away from your pain and place it back into your hands. The breakdowns you had in your car don't make you weak. The days you struggled just to get out of bed don't mean you aren't doing enough. Your progress today isn't diminished by your sorrow tomorrow. Those moments are another opportunity to learn, understand your triggers, and grow stronger. They're a reflection of what work you have yet to do, not the summation of who you are.

4) HEALING ISN'T FAIR.

To be honest, none of this is fair, is it? What was done to you wasn't fair. What was taken from you wasn't fair. The heartache you feel every day isn't fair. You and I both know that. You didn't deserve what they did to you, and you sure as hell don't deserve all that has come from it. I know you feel anger, resentment, and bitterness for those who put you here. That's normal. It's healthy even. Your emotions are something to guide you, not something you should rid yourself of. However, those feelings cannot erase what has been done. They cannot rewrite the past. Holding on to them is like drinking poison and expecting your abuser to die. That's why, as easy as it is to say, "healing isn't fair," just saying it isn't enough. You have to understand it, accept it, and then release it. It no longer serves a purpose in your life.

5) HEALING REQUIRES PERSEVERANCE, NOT PERFECTION.

Your greatest weapon in this battle you fight is your determination. You can show up tired. You can show up messy. You can show up scared. Just as long as you show up. There is no "right way" to heal. No one who has been down this road has followed a step-by-step or found their answers in a "healing for dummies" guide. We have all walked this road at our own pace. We have all followed our hearts and trusted our guts. We haven't healed while mimicking anyone else because that's not the way this works. My trauma is mine, just as your trauma is yours. My healing is mine, just as your healing is yours. The one common thread that weaves through every one of our journeys is that we have refused to give up. We haven't always walked with grace. Most days, we stumble through, guided only by our intuition and desire just to be better. We are clumsy. We are chaotic. We are confused. But we are constant. So, give yourself grace. Don't expect more than you have to give, and understand that what you have to give will vary by day. Remember that there is no room for perfection here. But there is unfathomable beauty in your grit.

Don't apologize for their actions.

We all do it. We all tend to feel guilt and shame for the results of someone else's actions. But why? Why do we rush to take responsibility that isn't ours? Stop it. Stop it right now. Guilt and shame do not serve you in this new chapter. You did not choose those things, and you can stop continuing to live in their aftermath now. No, you did not choose it then, but you are choosing it now. I know that's a hard pill to swallow. But I've had to swallow it over and over and over again.

Guilt and shame were used to control you then, so why would you think they wouldn't control you now?

You can feel sorrow and remorse for the mistakes you make because you are human, and you will continue to make mistakes. But take accountability, do the work, and move forward. Do not spend any more of your precious time stuck in the cycle that has hurt you for so long. You had no control over what they did then, so you hold no responsibility for the guilt now.

They should be ashamed. They are the abusers.

You should let that shit go, or you will continue to be their victim.

You were programmed to be the perfect victim. You decide when it's your time to reprogram.

I was asked recently why someone who had been through the things that I have would do some of the things they do. To clarify, someone I love deeply, who did not experience childhood sexual abuse, desperately wants to understand the actions of someone they care about deeply, who is a survivor. We talked for hours. They asked me questions without holding back, and I spoke with no hesitation or filter. It's amazing what a space filled with love and compassion can do for you.

This conversation and the thoughts shared have stuck with me.

Why do some survivors struggle to accept that what they went through was abuse, not love?

Why do some survivors compare their current healthy relationships to the relationships they had with their abusers and often treat their partner as if they are somehow inadequate compared to their abuser?

Why do some survivors develop a desire to sexually recreate some of the situations they faced during their abuse?

I can only imagine how hard it is for someone who has not lived through these things to understand how and why we survivors see the world the way we do. I feel as though I can see and understand both sides now that I have come so far in my healing. So, I hope to shed at least a little light on these questions and maybe build a bridge for understanding between survivors and their loved ones. Hypotheticals won't do here, so as difficult as it is, I'm going to use my personal experiences as an example to help show the whole picture.

Think back to when you were a child. Everything you learned, you learned through experience, from how to walk to what foods you like and everything in between. You learned that it hurt when you fell off your bike and that it was fun to play tag with your friends. As a child, while I was learning the normal childhood lessons, I was also being told that being forced to perform sexual acts was okay, that the pain and fear I felt was, in fact, love, and that pleasing my abusers was all I was good for. As a child whose brain was still developing, hearing these things repeatedly actually rewired the way my brain worked. I'm not a doctor, nor do I claim to understand enough of the science of it to explain thoroughly, but I am a survivor who spent years wondering why I would continue to search out the same abusive patterns and behaviors, knowing damn well they hurt like hell.

The childhood years are the most formative in brain development and function. During these years, your brain is building road after road inside itself, connecting thoughts, feelings, and actions. My abuse literally changed the way my brain grew. "Someone holding you down and forcing themselves on you" and "love" are two thoughts that do not connect logically. Looking at it from where I am today, I understand that. That in no way, shape, or form was any of it anything other than abuse. However, during the years I spent when my trauma brain was very much in control, these thoughts made perfect sense. This man LOVED me. He said so. He is supposed to. So, this MUST be love. Over time, that road inside my brain was built, brick by brick. Every time he hurt me and called it love, every time he manipulated, guilted, or shamed me, another brick was laid inside the very core of who I was. I didn't have enough life experience prior to my abuse to tell me these were all lies. I didn't have a "what love is" road previously built inside of me.

These were new bricks, new pathways, the first foundation established within me. The years of continued abuse reinforced these beliefs, and they carried through my adolescent years and into adulthood. It took years of therapy, soul searching, struggle, and growth to understand why these warped and unhealthy views of sex, love, and intimacy had become the truth for me. I slowly took apart that road the same way it had been laid, brick by brick. I realized I was worth far more than just sex. There goes a brick. I learned that love does not include manipulation or coercion. Another brick is gone. I accepted that what I had been through was, in fact, abuse, and I was the victim. Rip that one away.

Kadi and fiancé Matt, as Prince Charming and Cinderella, 2023

As I demolished that road, built decades ago, I replaced it with my own. Painstakingly slowly, I raised a new road. As I did, I realized I had to choose between allowing my trauma brain to take the lead still or giving power to my healing brain. I knew I couldn't have both. Your trauma brain is a selfish bastard and will not allow logic to reign alongside it.

If you are desperate to understand a survivor who does things like continue cycling in abusive relationships, compare partners to our abusers, or feel uncomfortable and out of place by any form of gentle and loving intimacy, remember that the logic you hold as true isn't a given for us. It's something we have to fight for.

YOU ARE NOT *NOTHING* WITHOUT YOUR TRAUMA

Read that again. You are NOT nothing without your trauma.

If you shed the things that were done to you, what's left? Are you afraid because you don't know? Been there. But I need you to hear me when I say that you are a whole, beautiful, worthy being. You don't have to know what you will look like after to begin shedding all of it now.

Here's a piece that I wrote when I began to accept this truth.

I can still hear her. Just the same as back then. She cries. She screams. She reaches out for love, but only he is there. She doesn't realize that it's all over. She doesn't see that she's safe now. I can still hear her deliberate breaths. I can still feel her heart racing until she vomits. It never ended for her. I reach out my hand to her, and she runs away. I try to hold her, to show her that she's worth so much more than what he's done, but her fear is her survival, so she hides. She buries herself so far down in hopes that he won't find her.

"13 years, sweet girl. It's been 13 years. He's gone." I whisper.

But it's no use. She believes the things he's said. She believes this is what she was made for. This is how she will make him love her. This is what little girls are supposed to do.

I tell her it's not. I try to show her the love she is worthy of. I screamed at her that it wasn't her fault.

"Please, please, come out," I begged her.

"The longer you stay, the more you hurt me."

I sob. I break. I Don't sleep.

"Let me show you your worth. Let me comfort you. Let me hold you and protect you."

She gives me the same answer she always does.

"No."

I feel anger begin to overtake me.

"If you do that, then I will break. I will be gone forever." Her voice cracks as she begins to run out of air.

"You are NOTHING without me," she screams, still hiding in the dark.

"This is what he made you. This is what you are. You do not exist without me. I'm sorry, but I can't go."

I reach out and touch her hand. She tries to rip it away.

I touch her face. I feel the swelling.

I touch her head, and I feel her confusion as it spins.

I look down. I see the blood. I feel her pain. I reach for a blanket, but there's nothing except her torn overalls.

I wrap my arms around her to keep her warm.

"You have to go. You need to be free. You are choosing to live in this darkness, and I cannot live here with you anymore."

She looks up at me, and I see that all that's left is empty fear.

"Please let me live. I will show him he was wrong. I need you to go so I can move on," I plead.

I think about how small she is. So fragile. So, innocent.

I put my forehead against hers, and I whisper, "I will always love you."

Light begins to overtake the shadows. Warmth begins to radiate inside of her. And for the first time, I can see how truly beautiful she is. How Truly beautiful I am.

It feels like a lifetime passes as I finally see past what he's done.

"It's time for me to go," she breathes as she fades into the light.

To "him"

My hatred for you disappears with her. I will forgive you. Not because you deserve it but because I do. I will no longer live as the broken, scared little girl you made me. I will no longer hate myself so that you can continue to rape me. I will no longer bathe in the guilt and shame for what YOU did. That part of me is gone. I am letting her go. Never again will you hold that power over me and suffocate me.

You may have gotten away with it for all those years, but you have no victory. For as much as you tried to bloody, beat, and break me, I still stand. Despite all the lies you made me believe, I know the truth.

I am worthy of love.

I am worthy of joy.

I am good for more than what you did to me.

I am not too damaged.

What you did is not love.

I do not have to carry this for the rest of my life.

You will answer for it someday. May God have mercy on your soul.

I was, am, and always will be a masterpiece. His actions change his existence, not mine. I had to let go of the suffocating hold that my trauma had on me to move forward and just look at what I have done now. I was never nothing. And as ironic as it is, letting go of the trauma made me so much MORE.

Don't spend precious time looking for answers that don't serve you.

I spent years wondering things such as, "Why me?" Not in the sense of a pity party. More in the sense of what was it about me that made Astaroth choose me? Obviously, I don't think like a pedophile, so I don't understand how their brains view attraction. I would never look at a child and think "sexy," so I often wonder how he could have looked at me and done exactly that. Further than the "Why," I have wondered the WHEN. When did he decide I was what he wanted? As I shared through these pages, his tactics were thoroughly thought out and planned. There was no part that

Kadi and Biological Dad at
Father-Daughter Ball, 2023

was a rash decision. So, at which moment was it that I changed from just a kid to his victim?

Here is a piece I wrote while I was still searching for these answers.

There was a beginning. There was a moment.
When was it?
When was the day you set your sights on me?
When was the day you chose me?

Write it down.
Say it out loud.

Mark the genesis.
Mark the birth of evil intentions.
Mark the onset of taking what was never given to you.
It was the dawn of my deliberate, lifetime death.

A lifetime war drenched in destruction: that's what you waged inside me.

Years of conflict. All yours.
So much bloodshed. All mine.

No angel resting on my shoulder. No devil on the other.
Only you.
Your vile words.
Your unclean hands.
Your hollow eyes.
Silencing me.

Every time you touched me, I thought, "This is it. This is the final battle. Survive this, and then you will have peace."

But you would have no ceasefire. You scoffed at the thought of peace.
My peace meant your misery.

Your victory meant my annihilation.

Even after I was rescued, when I was no longer your hostage, no longer under siege, you still remained.

You continued to exist in the moments I would wake, petrified at the thought of another attack.

You continued to exist in the days without rest, paralyzed by the barrage of guilt that was never mine to carry.

You continued to exist in the self-hatred that would swallow me up and tear me down with the strength of ten thousand bombs.

It would be the fight of my life, just to keep from ending mine.

Kadi, Kathi (Kadi's biological mom) and Annika,
3 generation photos, 2023, Jessica Simkin Photography

As you can see, I would never find the answers to those questions that I searched so fiercely for. Because they were answers only he has. But over time, I have come to understand that those answers don't have anything to do with my healing. They exist in their own space, in their own world, and my healing exists independently of them. I do not need to know his why or his when once I accept that it was never my fault. I never did anything to deserve the abuse. I never asked for it or caused it. In his warped, twisted, and demented reality, his actions were justified. But his reality isn't actuality.

I don't know the why or when of him choosing me. But I no longer feel the need to. Because I now know the why and when of something far greater: How I took everything that was done to me and everything that should have destroyed me and turned into one of the greatest victories of all time.

I'm Kadi. And despite all that I've been through and all that has been done to break me, I'm still an incredible mother, fiancé, daughter, sister, public speaker, and author.

Kadi speaking on stage at Rise Up conference, 2022, LevelUp Photography

Despite all the hatred shown to me throughout my life, I still care deeply and show it openly.

I am extra, I am loud, I am vibrant, and I am so full of love.

ACKNOWLEDGEMENTS

To Matt,

My greatest support and loudest cheerleader. There are not enough words to thank you for endless words of encouragement when I felt insufficient and for the love you poured into me, especially when I struggled the most. Thank you for lending me your strength without fail. You have always reminded me that I don't have to be perfect to be enough and that whatever I have to give is enough. Your steadfast, patient, and unconditional love has been one of the foremost reasons I have been able to take these pieces of me and put them onto these pages. You have loved me so fiercely that I have had no choice but to love myself. Thank you, thank you, thank you, for every second you have poured into me and into this book. I truly could not have done it without you. I love you more than I can say.

To my mother,

Thank you for always setting the example of strength. For all the times you feel like you failed, I see only perseverance and love. I didn't break this cycle. We broke it together. Because I truly could not have done it without all you have given me over the years. Many will never know the sacrifices you have made to protect me and love me throughout my life, but I will never forget. Thank you for all the ways you've helped me, spoken and unspoken. I love you.

To Tracy Ertl with Titletown Publishing,

There is no one I would rather have walking with me every step of the way through this process. Trusting you with this book was one of the best decisions I made through this process. You have inspired me, coached me, encouraged me, and have become a lifelong friend. I will never be able to thank you enough for all you have given to me, at any cost to yourself. I am so proud to have you listed on these pages. Thank you for believing in me.

To my family and friends who have supported and encouraged me,

Thank you for your love and motivation throughout this process. Thank you for standing by me through some of my toughest moments. Thank you for continuing to love me, even in the moments it may have been difficult. I have been absolutely blessed with an incredible support system, and I do not take any of you for granted.

To Lori Preuss,

Thank you for all of the late nights, rushed deadlines, and last-minute conference calls to bring this to life. Although a lot of your work was behind the scenes, it did not go unnoticed. Thank you for investing in me. This truly would not have been brought to life without you.

AFTERWORD

Kadi's story is a harrowing account of her experience with childhood sexual abuse and its long-reaching consequences. Reading Kadi's journey from strife to healing is a testament to her strength and resilience. I am confident that Kadi will lead others down a similar path of gaining their power back. The statistics of sexual violence in this country are appalling. Still, the good news is that because of extensive research on trauma and how it affects the body, we have evidence-based treatment options we know work to heal the body. Access to services and materials is more far-reaching than ever, making it easier to get help so no one must struggle with trauma alone. As a therapist, I would like to provide you with an understanding of the effects of sexual trauma on the body and offer you some additional resources to help you get started on your healing journey.

STATISTICS ON CHILDHOOD SEXUAL ABUSE (CSA)

Let's start with some sobering statistics. Kadi's story, sadly, is not uncommon. In the United States, one in 4 girls and one in six boys have experienced sexual abuse before the age of 18. According to the Department of Justice, a sexual assault is committed every 68 seconds, and every 9 minutes, the assault occurs against a child. The Rape, Abuse & Incest National Network (RAIIN), the largest anti-sexual violence organization in the United States, estimates that 25 out of every 1,000 children have experienced sexual abuse.

In one out of four cases, the child knows the perpetrator, and a stranger does not commit the act(s). 93% of child victims know their perpetrator, and 55% are sexually assaulted near or at their homes. Having a perpetrator who is a relative or family friend causes additional challenges, as the perpetrators often use threats of harm to other family members to keep their abuse a secret. Like Kadi's story, it is not uncommon for victims to be in adulthood before they remember and or disclose their abuse. Sometimes, when the abuse is disclosed, it is questioned or denied by a caregiver. Having little to no parental support or undisclosed abuse increases the probability of a broad array of mental health issues for the child. When sexual trauma remains unknown, the child misses out on the opportunity of having the support of an understanding caregiver who can intervene and provide support services that can assist in the healing process and mitigate the harmful long-term effects.

MENTAL HEALTH AFFECTS OF CHILDHOOD SEXUAL ABUSE

There is a plethora of research that shows that untreated childhood sexual abuse can have devastating consequences for a child's social and emotional development and directly impacts physical and mental health. Thanks to the research efforts of trauma experts like Bessel van der Kolk, Peter Levine, Peter Walker, Judith Lewis Herman, and Richard Schwartz, to just name a few, we now know that results of childhood sexual trauma can be stored in the body and hard-wired in the brain. If left untreated, symptoms can persist well into adulthood. Adult survivors of childhood sexual abuse have higher rates of anxiety, depression, post-traumatic stress disorder, substance abuse, eating disorders, body dysmorphia, dissociation, repression, somatic complaints, sleep disturbances, and sexual dysfunction than adults who haven't experienced it. Let's look at how some of these patterns of maladaptive functioning can develop.

When someone violates and betrays a child in such a profoundly violent way, it is a rational conclusion that the child learns to mistrust people. Pair this mistrust with a non-supportive caregiver who fails to intervene and protect the child; the view of the world as not a safe place intensifies. Perpetrators teach their victims to blur the boundaries between themselves and others, which interrupts the development of a strong sense of self/identity. Automatic biological body responses a child may have to the abuse may be confused as arousal and can lead a child into not trusting themselves or their feelings, blaming themselves for the abuse, and internalizing negative thoughts about themselves. A child who takes on personal responsibility for the abuse can experience feelings of guilt, shame, and unworthiness. Body dysmorphia, eating disorders, and obesity are issues related to body image problems that can develop as children begin to associate their body or appearance with feeling dirty or ugly. Children learn they cannot trust their bodies or feelings and that they must deny or suppress emotions to keep themselves safe. Lacking personal boundaries, a strong sense of identity, and mistrusting people make it difficult for survivors to have stable relationships with others. As a society, we are created to be relational beings; it is why we have the gift of language, so we can relate, support, and care for one another. The inability to develop or grow relationships, paired with internalized negative thought patterns, can lead to isolation and, inevitably, symptoms of depression. Depression is the most common long-term symptom among survivors of childhood sexual abuse. Research shows that survivors display more self-destructive behaviors, self-harm, and suicidal thoughts and actions than those who have not experienced this kind of abuse. Let's pause to discuss the gravity of this last statement.

SUICIDE AND SELF-HARM

In Kadi's story, she mentions that she used self-harm as a tool to regulate her emotions and had some suicidal thoughts. As a therapist and a researcher, I have seen the data that reports that being exposed to information about self-harm and suicide has a contagious effect. Simply put, when people are in pain and looking for ways to stop it and don't have many, it is natural to latch on to ideas and behaviors that seem to be working for others. In this information age, where the internet, social media, and streaming platforms have content available 24/7 at your fingertips, it can be a dangerous tool. Suicide is not a solution to any problem; the only thing it accomplishes is taking away the possibility of the situation being able to change for the better. There is only one you in this world, and the universe will not be the same without you. I know it sounds cliché because it is, and it also rings true. If you are at this stage in life, please reach out to a licensed mental health therapist to use some of the resources I have provided for you. You are not alone!

Self-harm is when a person intentionally destroys their body tissue as a coping mechanism for dealing with psychological pain. Self-harm can look like cutting, burning, piercing the skin, breaking, smashing, or dislocating bones, or hitting or punching yourself or objects. Other names for self-harm are cutting, non-suicidal self-injury, or self-mutilation. Self-harm is a very complex subject that is still being rigorously studied. One theory for why people choose it as a tool is because it is not easy to distract or turn off emotional pain.

In contrast, physical pain caused by self-harm is easily altered by halting the behavior. There is even some research that suggests there is an area of the brain where physical pain and emotional pain overlap neurologically, so when physical pain is present, it alters or decreases the emotional pain. Some of the more common reasons reported by people engaging in self-harm are decreasing feelings of numbness, dissociation, anger, or emotional pain, reducing stress, blocking flashbacks or painful memories, a distress signal for needing help or eliciting the support of others to feel cared for, a way to punish themselves and avoid punishing others. Self-harm is a maladaptive tool, kind of like using a sledgehammer to hang a picture frame on the wall. It may do the job, but it leaves behind a lot of damage. Self-harm is dangerous physically; you have the potential for permanent scars, infections, and uncontrollable bleeding. Endorphins are produced in your body as a response to physical pain as a numbing agent that has several disastrous consequences. First, seeking endorphin relief can create an addiction to self-harm as the body builds a tolerance to the endorphins. More frequent and intense harm will be needed to achieve the same results, which can result in life-threatening injuries.

Additionally, the more a person participates in self-harm, the more the inhibition or restraint around ideas of going through with an act of suicide is lifted. To be clear, self-harm and suicidal ideation are not the same; self-harm is considered an alternative to suicide and does not necessarily cause suicidal thoughts and behaviors. However, studies have shown that self-harm is related to successful suicide completion since it provides practice in overcoming psychological and physical barriers to damaging the body. Research shows that self-harm behavior has emotional effects as well; it intensifies feelings of guilt, shame, helplessness, and worthiness and diminishes your sense of identity. Hiding or having to lie about injuries creates internal issues that can have devastating consequences on your social life. Self-harm behaviors can make people avoid friends and family. They may even experience being stigmatized by loved ones who don't understand self-harm behaviors. Better coping tools are available that don't have the consequences of scars or the judgment of others who don't know what you are struggling with. Let a licensed therapist or a healer in your community show you how to put down that sledgehammer and pick up a better tool. I have provided other contact resources at the end of this afterword. Let's examine some of the different ways sexual trauma can present as long-term mental health symptoms.

SOMATIZATION

Somatization is best explained as a physical manifestation of pain that is essentially frozen or trapped in the body as a result of trauma and the psychological and or emotional stress it causes. The most widely reported somatic symptom survivors of sexual abuse report is pelvic pain. Somatic complaints, to name a few, can feel like headaches, difficulty swallowing, and gastrointestinal problems. Research reports that survivors have significantly more medical problems when compared to people who have not experienced sexual abuse, such as chronic anxiety, pain attack attacks, phobias, and post-traumatic stress disorder (PTSD). As you can see, traumatic thoughts, feelings, memories, or sensations can be deeply buried in parts of our brain and come out in different ways that seem entirely unrelated. What happens when our conscious mind doesn't remember?

Kadi recounts how she didn't remember her trauma until she was in her adulthood, which may sound very unusual to someone who hasn't experienced trauma. Let's look at how that may happen; remember, I am not diagnosing Kadi, just offering insight based on what the research says regarding trauma.

DISSOCIATION

A natural response to the trauma symptoms a person might experience during sexual abuse is dissociation. Dissociation is essentially the brain's way of protecting itself by disconnecting from the thoughts, feelings, memories, or sensations associated with the abuse. Sometimes, disconnection happens in a way that can be perceived as watching someone else go through the abuse; this is called depersonalization. A similar symptom, derealization, occurs when a person struggles to gauge reality accurately. Derealization can affect how a person perceives time, spatial reasoning, and distance. A person experiencing derealization may feel like they are viewing life through a dirty window or on a foggy day. Derealization often has people questioning the "realness" of what is happening within and around them.

Dissociative amnesia is the most common symptom of dissociation, and it occurs when the brain blocks out or represses information associated with the trauma. Dissociative Amnesia may look like difficulty when trying to call certain parts of childhood, having large gaps in memories, losing significant blocks of time, feelings of disorientation or confusion, nightmares and or flashbacks, difficulty experiencing feelings, or negating the effects or impact of the abuse. Depersonalization, derealization, and dissociative amnesia can be symptoms of childhood sexual abuse on their own, in conjunction with each other, or they can develop in a way that meets the criteria for a mental health diagnosis through the Diagnostic and Statistical Manual (DSM) the standardized manual that clinicians use to form a diagnosis. I want to take a moment to talk about the diagnosis formerly known as Multiple Personality Disorder because it is often represented negatively in the media, inadvertently causing myths and misconceptions about the diagnosis that continue the widespread stigmatization of people with Dissociative Identity Disorder (DID). Erroneous information exists not only in the public sector but aspects of academia and mental health are poisoned with the inaccuracies of the media's portrayals of what DID looks like. The dissemination of inaccurate information ultimately hurts the community of people who need support the most, the ones living with dissociation, so I want to make an effort to provide some education on the subject.

To deliver this information in the most accurate way possible, I will defer the definition of the diagnosis to two well-known sources in the field. The first source, An Infinite Mind, is a non-profit dedicated to supporting those living with dissociation and their caregivers and educating clinicians about dissociation. Dr. Jamie Marich, a clinical trauma specialist, has written an excellent resource book, *Dissociation Made Simple: A Stigma-free Guide to Embracing Your Dissociative Mind and Navigating Daily Life,* that I highly recommend for a comprehensive review of the subject. Multiple personality disorder is now known in the DSM-V as Dissociative Identity Disorder; as discussed previously, it develops as a childhood coping mechanism in response to trauma.

As a way to escape physical and emotional pain, the mind disconnects from the child and their sense of identity. The mind then compartmentalizes feelings, personality traits, characteristics, and memories associated with the event into a separate identity that develops into unique personality states. Each identity may have its own name and personal history. These personality states can take control of the individual's behavior at times and are followed by the person losing a block of time. These episodes of lost time are too extensive to be explained by ordinary forgetfulness. DID is a spectrum disorder with varying degrees of severity.

In some cases, certain parts of a person's personality are aware of important personal information, whereas other personalities are unaware. Some personalities appear to know and interact with one another in an elaborate inner world. In other cases, a person with DID may be completely aware of all parts of their internal system.

My descriptions of dissociation are a brief and watered-down version of these complex symptoms, meant to provide validation to those who may experience these symptoms as normative, possible responses to childhood sexual trauma. If you find any of these symptoms relatable, please dive deeper into the discussion surrounding dissociation through An Infinite Mind's website https://www.aninfinitemind.org/, where you can discover resources, monthly speaker series, and information about their annual conference. An Infinite Mind also provides a therapist directory for professionals trained in working with trauma and DID. Since I mentioned trauma several times, let's explore the meaning, as this is another "therapy buzzword" that is often used out of context.

TRAUMA

The word trauma was derived from the Greek trauma (τραύμα) tramatikos, which translates to trauma wound. In Greek, trauma refers to a physical wound or flesh injury. Mental health professionals use the term more broadly, including other adverse injuries, such as those that affect the psychological, emotional, social, and spiritual domains of functioning. The American Psychological Association (APA) defines trauma as "an emotional response to a terrible event like an accident, crime, or natural disaster." What an individual deems traumatic is subjective; what one person considers traumatic might not affect another similarly. A person's support system and other mitigating factors play a big part in their resilience, allowing healing to occur more quickly. Short-term responses to trauma might look like shock or denial. Short-term symptoms tend to improve over time, but sometimes, those symptoms can stick around and cause problems. Experiencing trauma activates the alarm system in our bodies, preparing and engaging parts needed for the survival response. When the brain gets overwhelmed with trauma, it can be challenging for the body to return to its "rest and relax" state. The mind can get trapped in a heightened state of arousal that has them experiencing fear in real-time, well after the trauma event. Unresolved trauma can feel like living in constant danger or under threat, causing hypervigilance, nightmares, or flashbacks, being irritated or constantly on edge, having trouble concentrating, insomnia, being easily startled, and engaging in risky behavior. These symptoms compromise the individual's ability to function daily. One study found that adult survivors of childhood sexual abuse have symptoms comparable to those of Vietnam War veterans.

TYPES OF TRAUMA

Clinically, trauma is broken down into three types. Acute trauma occurs from a one-time event, such as witnessing someone's death or being involved in a car accident. Chronic trauma differs as it is a series of events that occur over a long period of time, such as domestic violence, child abuse, or what a soldier might experience during a war. Complex trauma happens when an individual is exposed to multiple traumas over an extended period of time; these events are severe and unescapable and have broad, long-term effects. Complex trauma is often an aggressive violation of the victim, occurs in the context of a relationship, and has comprehensive and long-lasting impacts. Between 1995 and 1997, the Centers for Disease Control (CDC) and Kaiser Permanente conducted an adverse childhood experiences (ACE) study. Led by Vincent Felitti, the ACE study is one of the largest pieces of research we have to date on the relationship between the role of complex trauma in children and the ways it can negatively impact adulthood.

ADVERSE CHILDHOOD EXPERIENCES (ACES)

The ACE questionnaire features ten questions that focus on three areas of childhood adversity: physical and emotional abuse, neglect, and behaviors that interrupt household functioning (i.e., domestic violence, substance abuse, and incarceration). The study published a set of findings that revealed a strong relationship between multiple childhood adverse experiences, negative health outcomes in adulthood, and the ways these outcomes are created. ACE research data outcomes have helped the medical field generate a model called the ACE Pyramid that helps to explain these phenomena. The model theorizes that ACEs interrupt brain development in children, directly impacting social, emotional, and cognitive development. In response to toxic stress, many individuals develop coping skills that are considered to be risky behaviors. Engaging in risky behaviors exposes people to harm and threatens mortality. The ACE study has made a connection between individuals with ACE scores of 4 or more and mental health problems, disease, chronic physical health problems, disabilities, social struggles, and revictimization in adulthood. For example, having an ACE score of 4 is significantly linked with an increased risk of cancer, diabetes, heart disease, autoimmune disorders, COPD, stroke, Alzheimer's and Dementia, and suicide. For female victims of childhood sexual abuse, a high ACE score increases their risk of sexual violence and revictimization as much as 2-13 times. It increases the likelihood of non-sexual intimate partner violence by two times. Childhood sexual abuse effects are long-reaching and consist of much more than just mental health issues.

While this list of the relationship between childhood sexual abuse and long-term effect variables seems to be long, it is by no means exhaustive, nor will every victim experience and respond to the abuse in the same manner. Everyone's response to trauma is different, and every healing journey is unique. The purpose of this discussion is to convey two messages. All of these symptoms, expected and normal, are responses to childhood trauma. You are so much more than the "research," more than the coping mechanisms that you have had to adopt to get through what has been done to you. The good news is that there are so many ways for you to heal from trauma when you are ready! Being aware of your symptoms enables you to reach out for support and connect with the right resources to get you started on your healing journey. Symptoms are like landmarks; clinicians can use them to create roadmaps that help you reach your final destination without missing a significant view along the way. There are a variety of therapeutic mind-body connection resources available. EDMR and Somatic Experiencing Therapy are evidence-based trauma treatment models. Others are known as Complimentary Alternative Medicine (CAM), such as expressive art therapy, which includes Trauma-Focused Yoga, dance, art, and music therapies. CAM therapies also have research showing they are practical tools for healing trauma.

MIND-BODY CONNECTION THERAPIES

Researchers have begun to explore mind-body practices as an additional way to address the intense emotional scars and somatic symptoms that trauma leaves behind. The techniques and framework for these therapies emphasize increasing mindfulness to strengthen awareness. Mindfulness intentionally focuses on feelings and sensations inside the body and observing what is happening outside. The basis of the mind-body connection is that once awareness is present, tools such as body movement, guided imagery, deep breathing, and other relaxation techniques can train the mind to alter its physical functioning.

Emphasizing being in the present moment while focusing on the body can restore interoceptive awareness, our body's physical cues such as hunger, sleepiness, and thirst. Interoceptive awareness can be damaged by childhood trauma when children have to dissociate, avoid, or hide their feelings or physical needs to survive ongoing trauma. Disconnection from interceptive awareness interferes with the mind's ability to set appropriate boundaries and attend to self-care needs. For example, lacking awareness of being full can lead to overeating or ignoring the signals of tiredness, leading to sleep deprivation. When basic human needs are not being met, the alarm signals in our brains get activated again, and symptoms increase. Strengthening interceptive awareness helps the mind recognize physical and emotional pain, build tolerance, and process sensations rather than employing an avoidance (dissociation) coping style. I emphasize Mind-body therapies in the next section over traditional talk therapy because they provide clients with the tools to reconnect and feel safe in their bodies. Talk therapy has its place in the healing arts. Still, it can be jarring if a client is exposed to disturbing memories and doesn't have any tools to regulate them. When looking for a trauma-informed therapist, I highly recommend asking questions about their experience working with trauma, their views and beliefs about trauma, and their training to ensure they are qualified to help you through your healing journey. The first mind-body connection therapy we will explore is EDMR.

EYE MOVEMENT DESENSITIZATION AND REPROCESSING (EDMR)

EMDR is a psychotherapy that uses the brain's natural self-healing mechanism to help the body heal from symptoms and emotional turmoil from trauma exposure. Trauma memories are thought to be stored in the right side of the brain and, as we have discussed previously, in the body. EDMR utilizes a mind-body connection to access those memories by stimulating the right and the left brain hemispheres, a process called bilateral stimulation. Bilateral stimulation can be achieved in a few ways: through eye movements focused on a beam of light or moving object, headphones that play a tone that moves from one ear to the next, or vibrating paddles you hold in your hands. The goal of accessing stored memories is to help you move through intense, triggering emotions and reprocess them in ways that shift your thoughts. Reprocessing is done by pairing the memory with the resources and resiliency you already possess. Triggering events that signal the body to turn on the alarm bells (fight, flight, or freeze) are desensitized, releasing stored energy in the body. When used in the context of childhood sexual abuse, EDMR can undo the programming, false beliefs, and distorted thinking that developed as the result of the perpetrator's grooming. For example, EDMR can help you change negative thoughts about your level of responsibility for the abuse, how you view your body, and feelings of shame and confusion, and can transform them into more accurate and positive beliefs that will help you get your power back. In EDMR, you have control over the therapeutic process, as you are the one who processes the events; the therapist is only a guide to help you move toward healing. You get to take back the power and control that was taken from you during your trauma, which is healing in itself. Another option for addressing traumatic memories that are stored in the body that is less directive is called Somatic Experiencing Therapy (SET).

SOMATIC EXPERIENCING THERAPY (SET)

Somatic Experiencing Therapy (SET), like EDMR, is a therapeutic approach that utilizes the mind-body connection. Dr. Peter Levine, a leading trauma researcher, developed SET to address the physical and emotional pain that is "frozen or stuck" in the body as a result of trauma exposure. SET uses mindfulness, guided breathing, body awareness, and movement to process and release frozen trauma energy in the body so individuals can move toward healing. For survivors of childhood sexual abuse, being able to reconnect with their body and their emotions as a vessel of safety and containment, rather than fear and chaos, helps to rebalance their nervous system so they can cope with stress more effectively. Another therapy that allows clients to reclaim their bodies is Trauma-Focused Yoga.

TRAUMA-FOCUSED YOGA

Trauma-Focused Yoga is another type of therapy that uses the mind-body connection to heal trauma symptoms. Trauma-Focused Yoga is based on Hatha yoga principles. Hatha yoga uses physical movement and controlled breathing exercises to promote relaxation and increase mindfulness. Trauma-Focused Yoga differs from traditional yoga practices in the client's level of control. A trauma-informed Yogi will not physically guide clients into proper positioning; instead, the emphasis is on helping the client learn how to reconnect and build strength and mastery in their bodies. Learning to ground themselves in the moment, be comfortable, feel safe and stable in their bodies, and connect to the self-facilitates trust that fosters and strengthens their relationships with others. Trauma-Focused Yoga is also considered an expressive art therapy because of how the body movements of yoga can be used to express emotion, similar to dance.

EXPRESSIVE ART THERAPIES

Expressive Art Therapies can be defined as using different types of art: music, drawing, painting, sculpting, drama, and dance to experience and express feelings in a safe and supportive environment. Sand tray therapy is an accepted tool by clinicians to help clients become aware of how they view themselves in a non-threatening way. There is a ton of research showing that expressive arts such as drum circles, interpretive dance, and psychodramas help trauma victims connect with strong emotions, expel negative energy, improve social, and create supportive communities in the context of group therapy. Animal-assisted therapies incorporating trained animals such as a dog or horse have been promoted as safe ways to create a safe environment conveying acceptance and trust. Animals offer unconditional love and support that can make it easier to talk about the trauma.

There are many ways to get you on your healing journey and to strengthen mindfulness. There are a variety of talk therapy models that are evidence-based for treating trauma and include mindfulness-based psychotherapy approaches. To learn more about these approaches, refer to Dialectical Behavior Therapy (DBT), Acceptance and Commitment Therapy (ACT), and Mindfulness-Based Stress Reduction (MBSR). Lastly, I want to acknowledge that I am presenting very Western ideas of how to treat trauma, which might not work for everyone. Culturally diverse practices such as ayurvedic medicine, acupuncture, massage, prayer circles, oral storytelling, and energy work all have a place in healing. Traditional healers such as shamanism, practitioners, and other culturally diverse healers also have a place in this arena. Finding support in your household, particularly if you are blessed with having multiple generations available, or creating kinship bonds also helps promote resilience. Where you start your journey isn't as important as having the courage to start it. Where Kadi's story provided you hope for recovery, I intended to give you the information and the resources you need to join her on the road to healing. I wish you peace, comfort, and renewed strength to face the battle ahead. I am rooting for you and have complete confidence that you will be victorious; after all, you are a survivor.

AFTERWORD RESOURCES

CDC (2023, June 29). *Adverse Childhood Experiences (ACEs)*. Center for Disease Control and Prevention. Retrieved November 17, 2023, from https://www.cdc.gov/violenceprevention/aces/index. html

Center for Substance Abuse Treatment (U.S.). Trauma-Informed Care in Behavioral Health Services. Rockville (M.D.): Substance Abuse and Mental Health Services Administration (U.S.); 2014. (Treatment Improvement Protocol (TIP) Series, No. 57.) Section 1, A Review of the Literature. Available from: https://www.ncbi. nlm.nih.gov/books/NBK207192/

The Center for Youth Wellness (2017). *Childhood adversity increases the risk for long-term health and behavioral issues.* https://center-foryouthwellness.org/health-impacts/#:~:text=Experiencing%20 4%20or%20more%20ACEs,%2C%20diabetes%2C%20Alzhei-mers%20and%20suicide.

Crandall, A., Miller, J. R., Cheung, A., Novilla, L. K., Glade, R., Novilla, M. L. B., ... & Hanson, C. L. (2019). ACEs and counter-ACEs: How positive and negative childhood experiences influence adult health. *Child abuse & neglect, 96*, 104089.

Dietz, T. J., Davis, D., & Pennings, J. (2012). Evaluating animal-assisted therapy in group treatment for child sexual abuse. *Journal of child sexual abuse, 21*(6), 665-683.

Department of Justice, Office of Justice Programs, Bureau of Justice Statistics, Female Victims of Sexual Violence, 1994-2010 (2013)

Felitti, V.J., Anda, R.F., Nordenberg, D., Williamson, D.F., Spitz, A.M., Edwards, V., Koss, M.P., & Marks, S.J. (1998). Relationship of childhood abuse and household dysfunction to many of the leading causes of death in adults: The adverse childhood experiences (ACE) study. *American Journal of Preventive Medicine*. 14(4), 245-258.

Franklin, J. (2014). How does self-injury change feelings? *The Fact Sheet Series, Cornell Research Program on Self-Injury and Recovery*. Cornell University, Ithaca, NY.

Hall, M., & Hall, J. (2011). The long-term effects of childhood sexual abuse: Counseling implications. Retrieved from http://counseling-outfitters.com/vistas/vistas11/Article_19.pdf

H.M Zinzow, H.S. Resnick, J.L. McCauley, A.B. Amstadter, K.J. Ruggiero, & D.G. Kilpatrick, Prevalence and Risk of Psychiatric Disorders as a Function of Variant Rape Histories: Results From a National Survey of Women. *Social psychiatry and psychiatric epidemiology*, 47(6), 893-902 (2012).

Kessler, M. R. H., Nelson, B., Jurich, A., & White, M. (2004). Clinical decision-making strategies of marriage and family therapists in the treatment of adult childhood sexual abuse survivors. *American Journal of Family Therapy*, 32(1), 1-10.

Kilburn, E. & Whitlock, J.L. (2009). Distraction techniques and alternative coping strategies. The Practical Matters Series, Cornell Research Program on Self-Injury and Recovery. Cornell University. Ithaca, NY.

Kolaitis, G., & Olff, M. (2017). Psychotraumatology in Greece. *European Journal of Psychotraumatology*, 8(sup4), 135175. https://doi.org/10.1080/20008198.2017.1351757

Maltz, W. (2002). *Treating the sexual intimacy concerns of sexual abuse survivors*. Sexual and Relationship Therapy, 17(4), 321-327.

Price C. (2005). Body-oriented therapy in recovery from child sexual abuse: an efficacy study. *Alternative therapies in health and medicine, 11*(5), 46–57.

Ratican, K. (1992). Sexual abuse survivors: Identifying symptoms and special treatment considerations. *Journal of Counseling & Development*, 71(1), 33-38.

Struck, S., Stewart-Tufescu, A., Asmundson, A. J., Asmundson, G. G., & Afifi, T. O. (2021). Adverse childhood experiences (ACEs)

research: A bibliometric analysis of publication trends over the first 20 years. *Child Abuse & Neglect, 112,* 104895.

West, J., Liang, B., & Spinazzola, J. (2017). Trauma Sensitive Yoga as a complementary treatment for post-traumatic stress disorder: A Qualitative Descriptive analysis. *International journal of stress management, 24*(2), 173–195. https://doi.org/10.1037/str0000040

Whitlock, J., Minton, R., Babington, P., & Ernhout, C. (2015). The relationship between non-suicidal self-injury and suicide. *The Information Brief Series,* Cornell Research Program on Self-Injury and Recovery. Cornell University, Ithaca, NY.

CHILDHOOD SEXUAL ABUSE RESOURCES

THE NATIONAL CHILD TRAUMATIC STRESS NETWORK (NCTSN)

https://www.nctsn.org/what-is-child-trauma/trauma-types/sexual-abuse/nctsn-resources

RAPE, ABUSE & INCEST NATIONAL NETWORK (RAINN)

https://www.rainn.org/resources
Telephone hotline: 800-656-HOPE (4673)
RAINN offers a National Sexual Assault Hotline and a Helpline for Male Survivors, Online chat (also in Spanish) and a hotline, and its website provides a search bot for local providers trained in sexual trauma

www.1in6.org
www.takingbackourselves.org
www.joyfulheartfoundation.org
www.yesican.org
www.tmiproject.org

DISSOCIATION

An Infinite Mind (AIM)
A non-profit organization committed to helping people living with Dissociative Identities, their supporters, and therapists access to accurate information and provide a community of people who understand and live or work with people living with dissociation. Offering monthly speaker series and an annual conference.
https://www.aninfinitemind.org/

SELF-HARM RESOURCES

The Crisis Text Line
Serves young people in any type of crisis, providing them access to free, 24/7 emotional support and information they need.
https://www.crisistextline.org/help-for-self-harm/
Text CONNECT to 741741 to connect with a real human.
http://www.selfinjury.com
https://www.selfinjury.bctr.cornell.edu/resources.html
http://www.bbc.co.uk/health/conditions/mental_health/coping_skills.shtml
http://www.helpguide.org/mental/self_injury.htm

SUICIDE RESOURCES

The Centers for Disease Control and Prevention
A website on suicide injury and violence prevention, including research, publications, national statistics, prevention strategies and resources:
http://www.cdc.gov/violenceprevention/suicide/index.html
To speak to a skilled and trained crisis worker, Dial:
988 Suicide & Crisis Lifeline
988 Lifeline Options for Deaf and Hard of Hearing

For TTY Users: Use your preferred relay service or dial 711, then 988.

The National Suicide Prevention Lifeline

A 24-hour, toll-free, confidential suicide prevention hotline is available to anyone in suicidal crisis or emotional distress.

Dial 1-800-273-TALK (8255), the call will be routed to the nearest crisis center in a national network of more than 150 crisis centers.

The Lifeline's national network of local crisis centers provides crisis counseling and mental health referrals day and night: **http://www.suicidepreventionlifeline.org/**

The Trevor Project

The Trevor Project is the leading suicide prevention and crisis intervention non-profit organization for LGBTQ young people. We provide information & support to LGBTQ and young people 24/7, all year round. Hotline, online chat, and texting support are available.

https://www.thetrevorproject.org/

Call Us: 1-866-488-7386

Text Us: 678-678

Therapist Directories

https://directory.traumahealing.org/ (Somatic therapists)

https://www.emdria.org/find-an-emdr-therapist/ (EMDR Therapists)

https://www.havoca.org/resources/find-a-therapist/Help for Adult Victims Of Child Abuse

https://traumatherapistnetwork.com/

Take the ACES Quiz

https://developingchild.harvard.edu/media-coverage/take-the-ace-quiz-and-learn-what-it-does-and-doesnt-mean/

FURTHER READING

Carpenter, D. (2018). *Childhood Trauma and the Non-Alpha Male: Gender Role Conflict, Toxic Shame, and Complex Trauma: Finding Hope, Clarity, Healing, and Change.* Atlantic Publishing Group.

Schiraldi, G. (2021). *The Adverse Childhood Experiences Recovery Workbook: Heal the Hidden Wounds from Childhood Affecting Your Adult Mental and Physical Health.* New Harbinger Publications.

LePera, N. (2021). *How to do the work: recognize your patterns, heal from your past, and create yourself.* First edition. New York, NY, Harper Wave, an imprint of Harper Collins Publishers.

Levine, A. and Heller, R. (2010). *Attached: the new science of adult attachment and how it can help you find and keep love.* Penguin.

Levine, P. A. (2010). *In an unspoken voice: how the body releases trauma and restores goodness.* Berkeley, North Atlantic Books.

Levine, P. A. (1997). Waking the tiger: healing trauma: the innate capacity to transform overwhelming experiences. Berkeley, Calif., North Atlantic Books.

Nakazawa, D. J. (2016). *Childhood disrupted: how your biography becomes your biology, and how you can heal.* New York, Atria Paperback.

Schwartz, R. C. (2021). *No bad parts: healing trauma & restoring wholeness with the internal family systems model.* Sounds True.

Shershun.E. (2021). *Healing Sexual Trauma Workbook: Somatic Skills to Help You Feel Safe in Your Body, Create Boundaries, and Live with Resilience.* New Harbinger Publications.

van der Kolk, B. A. (2014). The body keeps the score: Brain, mind, and body in the healing of trauma. Viking.

Walker, P. (2013). *Complex PTSD: from surviving to thriving: a guide and map for recovering from childhood trauma.* First Edition. Lafayette, CA, Azure Coyote.

CONTRIBUTORS

FOREWORD BY DR. BONNIE NUSSBAUM

Dr. Bonnie Nussbaum is a holistic coach and clinical psychologist who believes people are capable of far more than they think they are. She is a down-to-earth person with an expansive energy. She invests a lot of herself in working with people, is highly committed to your success, and helps you commit to yourself at that same high level. She can create a big space for you to confront your major resistances and release the last big barriers to your inevitable success. She is a master of discernment, able to hit the core of what needs addressing, and has the tenacity to "go there" with you and the grit to get you through it.

https://www.empowermentandpurpose.com
https://www.facebook.com/bonnienussbaum/

AFTERWORD BY JENNIFER L. NAPIER, MA., LMFT

Jennifer Napier is a licensed Marriage and Family Therapist with a private practice in Casselberry, Florida, specializing in adolescent and child Therapy. She is a trauma-informed and trained therapist, which has culminated from her own experience as a survivor of childhood sexual abuse. She currently volunteers for An

Infinite Mind, an organization committed to supporting and educating those living with dissociative identity disorder. Other pursuits include finishing her doctorate and becoming a trauma-focused Yogi. She is a Breast Cancer Survivor, avid runner, and crafter and lives in Central Florida with her family.